Your Faith *and the* World Today

Your Faith *and the* World Today

Emails of Instruction and Encouragement to Young Christians

BRAD STETSON

WIPF & STOCK · Eugene, Oregon

YOUR FAITH AND THE WORLD TODAY
Emails of Instruction and Encouragement to Young Christians

Copyright © 2025 Brad Stetson. All rights reserved. Except for brief quotations in critical publications or reviews, no part of this book may be reproduced in any manner without prior written permission from the publisher. Write: Permissions, Wipf and Stock Publishers, 199 W. 8th Ave., Suite 3, Eugene, OR 97401.

Wipf & Stock
An Imprint of Wipf and Stock Publishers
199 W. 8th Ave., Suite 3
Eugene, OR 97401

www.wipfandstock.com

PAPERBACK ISBN: 979-8-3852-6342-4
HARDCOVER ISBN: 979-8-3852-6343-1
EBOOK ISBN: 979-8-3852-6344-8

VERSION NUMBER 11/20/25

Scripture quotations taken from The Holy Bible, New International Version®, NIV®. Copyright © 1973, 1978, 1984, 2011 by Biblica, Inc. Used with permission of Zondervan. All rights reserved worldwide. www.zondervan.com

For Sam, the son I prayed for, and whom I love

"I don't want my ideas to die with me."
—Temple Grandin

Contents

Preface | ix
A Word to the Reader | xi
Introduction | xiii
Also From Brad Stetson | xvi

Part I: Theological Topics

1. Christology: Who Is Jesus Christ? | 3
2. Prayer | 12
3. Hypocrisy | 25
4. Evangelism | 33
5. Grief | 50
6. Music | 61
7. The Demonic | 67

Part II: Social and Ethical Topics

8. Politics | 77
9. Abortion | 83
10. Honoring Parents | 92
11. Dating and Marriage | 97
12. Sex and Sexuality | 103

13 Alcohol and Drugs | 111

14 Television and Media | 118

15 Race | 124

Appendix A: 12 Breath Prayers and Declarations, and a Daily Prayer of Committal | 131

Appendix B: Dietrich Bonhoeffer's Legacy for Americans Today | 133

Bibliography | 137

Preface

When I was a prison chaplain in the 1980s and 1990s, I would tell the men that their Christian faith was a 24/7 calling: It was a full-time commitment that was meant to shape their lives all day, everyday. When I was a professor at Christian colleges in the 1990s and 2000s, I told my students the same thing: Their faith was for every area of life and living, not just Sundays or chapel services.

Both groups of people, it seems to me, uneasily wondered if their faith could pervade every behavioral and intellectual dimension of their life. Perhaps influences in their lives or their own experiences suggested to them that it couldn't, but when I stressed to them that their faith equipped them with the strength and insight they would need for all of life—every season, every experience, every endeavor—they took heart, they were encouraged, and they were strengthened.

I hope this book has the same effect on you, irrespective of your stage in the Christian life. Although I've addressed this book to young Christians, it's relevant for all of us, and it speaks to our common Christian experience. Part devotional, part apologetic, part exhortation, and part social criticism, this book touches on all of life, and urges the reader to go further and fully take hold of a rigorous Christian worldview in every topic it discusses, and each issue of life it considers.

Christians won't always draw the same inferences from their faith and the Scriptures regarding every topic of life, and of course there are myriad styles or traditions of Christian faith and practice,

Preface

from Orthodox to charismatic to a lot in between. So certainly there is not one single Christian worldview, the same in every detail for everyone. But if a worldview is to be authentically Christian, it must start with Jesus Christ, the God-man, and take his claims about himself and us seriously. And from there, so much else falls into place. This book models that reality.

The loving Trinitarian God of the Bible has called us to himself through the incarnation of God the Son, and through the Scriptures that reveal him. As we respond to that sacred call, we will joyfully live out our faith, and find that it encompasses a view of the world—our world—which is at once true to the objective facts of reality, and true to the subjective sentiments of our own individual human experience. May each day that we live confirm that consonance. *In Deum semper auctus!* (Always growing in God!)

A Word to the Reader

THIS BOOK CAN BE read straight through, or in stand-alone chapters as encouraging exhortations to think, from a Christian point of view, on the topic at hand.

Each chapter begins with three epigrams, mainly from C. S. Lewis, that serve as reflective prompts, inviting you, the reader, to begin thinking about the topic of that chapter. At the end of each chapter is a reference to an inspiring song on Youtube which complements that discussion. I urge you to listen to each song and savor its message. After the song is a brief prayer asking for God's guidance on that chapter's topic, and also a relevant Scripture passage to memorize. At the end of each chapter are five carefully selected suggested readings. These books will lead you into a deeper biblical and intellectual engagement with the subject of that chapter, and greatly assist you in developing your Christian worldview on that issue, and on your life as a whole.

Introduction

As I drove home late that night after my talk, I thought to myself, "What a disaster!" Everything that could go wrong, did go wrong. The host mispronounced my name, the microphone cut in and out the whole night, and my PowerPoint slideshow—meticulously prepared down to the sound clips and font size of the text on the slides—didn't work at all. The only image projected on the screen the entire length of my speech was my email address. I'd spent hours on that PowerPoint, and was so proud of it. I still can't believe it didn't work during my talk, as I'd tested it out when I first got to the auditorium, and it worked fine then. The poor guy who was my host—a sophomore student named Blaine who was a fine arts major—knew nothing about the computer or sound systems, so he wasn't much help. He also had the unfortunate habit of never looking at me when he spoke. Not once did he raise his eyes from his iPhone and look straight at me. The closest he came was a sheepish grin in my direction after he mispronounced my last name as he shuffled off the stage after introducing me.

I was the first chapel speaker of the new semester at the large Christian college near my house, and I was happy to be there. I was a last-minute substitution for whoever they had scheduled, a person who, I was told, had just tested positive for COVID-19. But I didn't mind being a fill-in speaker. I had been wanting to talk to a gathering of young Christians for a long time, and I'd been relentlessly pestering the chapel director at this particular school, asking for a chance to talk to the students.

Introduction

I had taught at a few Christian colleges some years earlier, and I was bothered by the experience. Maybe my expectations had been unrealistic, but most of the students I had didn't seem too interested in the gospel and integrating their Christian faith into their university education. They were just looking for a convenient place to earn a degree. When it came to their faith they seemed only to be going through the motions. The Christian university I had taught the longest at, about six years, allowed up to 15 percent of the student body to be non-Christians, and the other 85 percent were not exactly Billy Graham. Really, they didn't seem much different from the students I had taught at the sprawling state university nearby.

So even though those earlier experiences with young Christians were disappointing, I still felt an urgency to talk to them about their faith and the world today. In fact, maybe it was because it seemed to me they were so apathetic about their Christian faith and worldview, I wanted to share with them that their Christian faith is in fact up to the challenges of contemporary life. I wanted to tell young believers that they carried within them the antidote to the poisons that polluted the people and institutions around them in their world. I wanted to say to them that the message of Jesus that they believed was the only message that could bring real meaning and deep purpose to human life—theirs and others. I wanted to remind them that the truth of Jesus' words in John 10:10, "I have come that [you] might have life, and have it abundantly," was as urgent today as it was the day he spoke it. I wanted them to know that in Christ, they were deeply loved and known, and that he had brought them to this place in their life on purpose, for a purpose.

As I drove into my driveway, arriving home, I turned the car off and sat silently for a minute. I recalled the faces of the students sitting in the audience listening to me. They looked so young, so vulnerable at the outset of their lives. Some of them seemed truly curious. Maybe it was providential, I thought, that my vaunted PowerPoint presentation didn't work, and that the only image the students could look at for forty-five minutes was my email address.

INTRODUCTION

Maybe some of these young Christians would reach out to me and share their ideas, or ask me a question. I hope they do, I thought. I have more I want to say to them. I want to encourage them. "Lord please bring it to pass," I whispered.

Also From Brad Stetson

Challenging the Civil Rights Establishment: Profiles of a New Black Vanguard (with Joseph G. Conti), 1993.

Pluralism and Particularity in Religious Belief, 1994.

The Silent Subject: Reflections on the Unborn in American Culture (Editor), 1996.

Black and Right: The Bold New Voice of Black Conservatives in America (Co-Edited with Joseph G. Conti and Stan Faryna), 1997.

Human Dignity and Contemporary Liberalism, 1998.

Tender Fingerprints: A True Story of Loss and Resolution, 1999.

From Rage to Responsibility: Black Conservative Jesse Lee Peterson and America Today (with Jesse Lee Peterson), 2000.

Living Victims, Stolen Lives: Parents of Murdered Children Speak to America, 2003.

The Truth About Tolerance: Pluralism, Diversity and the Culture Wars (with Joseph G. Conti), 2005.

Jewish Sacred Music and Jewish Identity: Continuity and Fragmentation (Co-Edited with Jonathan L. Friedmann), 2008.

Choosing to Survive: Loved Ones of Murder Victims Tell Their Stories (Editor), 2017.

PART I

Theological Topics

1

Christology
Who Is Jesus Christ?

"It is by far the most amazing miracle in the whole Bible—far more amazing than the resurrection and more amazing than the creation of the universe. The fact that the infinite, omnipotent, eternal Son of God could become man and join Himself to a human nature forever—so that infinite God became one person with finite man—will remain for eternity the most profound miracle and the most profound mystery in all the universe."

—Wayne Grudem

"I have read in Plato and Cicero sayings that are very wise and very beautiful, but I never read in either of them: 'Come unto me all ye that labor and are heavy laden.'"

—Augustine

"The Son of God became a man to enable men to become sons of God."
—C. S. Lewis

Part I: Theological Topics

From: thebradstetson@gmail.com
To: Mary

Thanks for your insightful note, Mary. You're right, I think, in pointing out that it is sometimes hard to separate the Jesus of Scripture from the Jesus of American culture. And you're also very astute to point out that accurately understanding the incarnation and Jesus' divinity is central to having an accurate understanding of the Christian faith. I mean, get Jesus wrong, and you'll likely get everything else wrong.

It is amazing, I think, that Jesus—as both a historical figure and as a focus of people's attention and imaginations—continues to generate so much concern and fascination. Here is a man who did not fade into history. To the contrary, he has essentially dictated history. I'm struck by the fact that in my lifetime alone so much popular culture has been devoted to him. I remember Franco Zefferelli's television drama from the 1970s, *Jesus of Nazareth*, and the Broadway show of the same time, *Jesus Christ Superstar*. Both were seminal cultural moments, and the music of *Jesus Christ Superstar* is still performed today. And then there was the controversial Martin Scorcese film, *The Last Temptation of Christ*, and later Mel Gibson's monumental film, *The Passion of the Christ*, with Gibson's film about the resurrection on the near horizon as I write this. People are still so compelled by this ancient carpenter from a small town in a distant outpost of the Roman Empire of 2,000 years ago that they write and think about him constantly.

Yes, from ancient and Renaissance art to all the great sculptures and paintings of the Western heritage to the epic films of Hollywood and contemporary retellings of the Jesus story, Jesus remains a central interest of people. Jesus' question to his disciples, "Who do you say that I am?" (Matt 16:15), has echoed within the hearts of men down through the centuries, and we hear it still.

There's a charming old essay that drives home to us the remarkable truth that Jesus' life, though extremely humble, has improbably become extremely influential. A passage of it reads:

> He was born in an obscure village, the child of a peasant woman. He grew up in still another village where he worked until he was thirty. . . . He never wrote a book. He never held an office. He never had a family or owned a home. He didn't go to college. He never travelled more than 200 miles from the place he was born. . . . He was nailed to the cross between two thieves. While he was dying his executioners gambled for his clothing, the only property he ever had. . . . Nineteen centuries have come and gone and today he is the central figure of the human race. . . . All the armies that ever marched, all the navies that ever sailed, all the parliaments that ever sat, all the kings that ever reigned, put together, have not affected the life of man on earth as much as that One Solitary Life.[1]

The New Testament certainly gives us a clear picture of Jesus' identity, this man who is the epicenter of history. He was born the son of David, the son of Abraham (Matt 1:1). He announced the coming of the kingdom of God (Matt 4:12–17). He successfully resisted every temptation of the devil (Luke 4:1–13). He commanded the wind and the water and he showed his mastery of the chemical elements by transforming water into wine (Luke 8:22–25; John 2:6–11). He pronounced the forgiveness of sins (Mark 2:1–12). He raised the dead and he himself came back to life after being dead for three days (John 11:38–44; 20:1–18). He claimed to be God, and proved it by his bodily resurrection.[2]

So, Mary, as all these verses indicate, and as the Christian church since its inception in the first century AD has declared, Jesus is God. Christian scholar Stephen Wellum puts the matter succinctly and comprehensively: "Jesus is God the Son, the second person of the eternal Trinity, who at a specific point in history took to himself a human nature and was born as Jesus of Nazareth in order to accomplish our redemption. In the language of the Chalcedonian Definition, our Lord Jesus is God the Son incarnate—one person who subsists in two natures, fully God and fully

---

1. Francis, *Real Jesus*, cited in Wellum, *God the Son Incarnate*, 35–36.
2. See Wellum, *God the Son Incarnate*, 36.

Part I: Theological Topics

man—who alone is Lord and Savior and worthy of our worship, trust and obedience."[3]

Jesus of Nazareth—Jesus Christ—is God the Son, the preincarnate and eternal Logos. He is also known sometimes as the cosmic Christ.[4] This is made clear in many New Testament passages, including famously John 1:1, 14, and in John 17:5, where Jesus says, "And now, Father glorify me in your presence with the glory I had with you before the world began." Jesus taught his own preexistence throughout the Gospel of John (John 3:13; 6:33, 38, 62; 8:23; 16:28). Jesus' very claim to divinity, which is all throughout the Gospels, clearly establishes his preexistence, since God (which he was and is) is by definition eternal and beyond time. He is self-existent, and without beginning or creation. Thus Jesus, as God the Son, had to exist forever—past, present, and future—and in fact beyond time itself.[5] Paul further reiterates the central and active role of Jesus as God the Son by highlighting his divine personal agency in creation by writing in Col 1:16–17: "For in him [i.e., Jesus] all things were created.... All things were created through him and for him. He is before all things, and in him all things hold together." See also John 1:3: "Through him [Jesus] all things were made."

Yes, God the Son took on human flesh, and became Jesus of Nazareth, always fully God and fully man. And, note Mary, Jesus did not become a man for just a little while. Jesus' preincarnate divine nature was, in the incarnation, permanently united to his human nature.[6] As theologian Wayne Grudem wrote, "[Jesus] lives forever not just as the eternal Son of God, the second person of the Trinity, but also as Jesus, the man who was born of Mary, and as Christ, the Messiah and Savior of his people. Jesus will remain

---

3. Wellum, *God the Son Incarnate*, 39–40.

4. These titles are applied to him depending on the context of discussion, but for a good discussion of these titles with respect to salvation, see Willard, "Apologetics in Action."

5. For much more biblical evidence along these lines, see Got Questions, "Does the Bible Support."

6. Grudem, *Systematic Theology*, 678.

CHRISTOLOGY

fully God and fully man yet one person forever."[7] The body he took on, with its crucifixion scars, will be an eternal testimony to his love for us.

Although these theological ideas are dense, Mary, every Christian should do his or her best to understand them. I've included below the Nicene Creed, which conveys the classic "Christology," the understanding of Jesus Christ that has always defined orthodox Christianity:

> I believe in one God, the Father Almighty, maker of heaven and earth and of all things visible and invisible. And in one Lord Jesus Christ, the only-begotten Son of God, begotten of His Father before all worlds, God of God, Light of Light, very God of very God, begotten, not made, being of one substance with the Father, by whom all things were made; who for us men and for our salvation came down from heaven and was incarnate by the Holy Spirit of the virgin Mary and was made man; and was crucified also for us under Pontius Pilate. He suffered and was buried. And the third day He rose again according to the Scriptures and ascended into heaven and sits at the right hand of the Father. And He will come again with glory to judge both the living and the dead, whose kingdom will have no end. And I believe in the Holy Spirit, the Lord and giver of life, who proceeds from the Father and the Son, who with the Father and the Son together is worshiped and glorified, who spoke by the prophets. And I believe in one holy catholic and apostolic Church. I acknowledge one Baptism for the remission of sins, and I look for the resurrection of the dead and the life of the world to come. Amen.[8]

So for the Christian today, in the twenty-first century, the doctrinal truths of the incarnation should translate into a simple and sustaining faith that says, "I am created by God, and because of my faith in the saving death and resurrection of his divine Son

---

7. Grudem, *Systematic Theology*, 678.
8. ZA Blog, "Nicene Creed." Note, "catholic" here with a small "c" denotes the Christian church universally.

Jesus Christ on the cross so long ago, I am going to live on in heaven, in God's kingdom, world without end."

You asked me, Mary, to give you an example of an apologetic you could offer your friends who aren't Christians, but are curious about Jesus. These next few paragraphs seem to me to be a useful tool you could use to suggest to your friends that they can know the truth about Jesus, and find in him life and peace.[9]

Time and time again, all throughout the Gospels, and time and time again, all throughout the New Testament, this message gets reiterated over and over: God sent his only Son to suffer a horrible death in our place—he paid the penalty we earned for our sins—and that by believing in him, relying on him, and accepting him as our Lord and Savior, we can be forgiven and granted everlasting life, life beyond the death of this physical body. As Peter the apostle told the ruling religious leaders of his day, "Salvation is found in no one else, for there is no other name under heaven given to men by which we must be saved" (Acts 4:12).

This idea of the person and work of Jesus Christ on the cross as the sole path of salvation for human beings is an idea that is offensive to the spirit of our times today. It is a stumbling block, and sometimes people wrongly even see it as intolerant.[10] People today generally desire to believe that all religious truth claims are equal, that whatever anyone wants to be true is true, and that there is no such thing as hell.[11] But just because we want something to be true, that doesn't make it so. Once the authority of Scripture is jettisoned, people will form beliefs based on their own desires or whatever ideas are dominant in their culture. Once people stop believing in the triune God of Scripture, uniquely revealed in Scripture, they don't believe in nothing, they believe in anything.

---

9. Examples of this kind of apologetic presentation abound. See McDowell, *New Evidence That Demands a Verdict*; Strobel, *Case For Christ*; Lewis, *Mere Christianity*; Montgomery, *Faith Founded on Fact*.

10. For extended discussion of this theme, see Stetson and Conti, *Truth About Tolerance*.

11. See my extended discussion of this topic in Stetson, *Pluralism and Particularity in Religious Belief*. Also see Walls, *Hell*.

The Christian message of salvation in Jesus alone is historically rooted. Jesus of Nazareth existed in first-century Palestine as a historical figure. He was a real person there. It's not just the New Testament documents that declare this. The Jewish historian Josephus, the Roman historians Tacitus and Pliny the Younger, and the record of archeology all mention Jesus the Nazarene and the fact he had followers who worshiped him as God.

You see Jesus himself claimed to be God incarnate, God become a man. He claimed to be the Lord himself, the God that the Jews worshiped. It is of course a stunning claim, and one that he supported by his resurrection from the dead after having been crucified. And it is evident that his followers believed him, and claimed to have witnessed him after his resurrection. And it is a historical fact that each of the apostles, in the months and years after Jesus' resurrection, were each eventually executed by various angry mobs, specifically for claiming Jesus had been risen from the dead. They were killed for this testimony—alone—and after having been given an opportunity to recant and deny that it was true. But they didn't deny it—they died for that belief, because they were convinced it was true. Now, even the most fervent follower might stick to what he knows to be a lie when other people are around watching, although it seems unlikely. But the apostles were killed years later, individually, far away from the communities and people they had first testified to about Jesus' resurrection. Clearly they were deeply committed to this belief; they were convinced he was Lord.

And each of us today, is faced with a decision about Jesus. Who was he? Was he the Lord, as he claimed? If not, he could only have been a terrible liar, or an outright lunatic. But the record of the rest of his life, of the conduct of his disciples at the time, and the remarkable, improbable growth of the Christian message through the centuries all make it so very unlikely that Jesus of Nazareth could have been a clever liar or a crazy man. This trilemma—Is Jesus Lord, liar, or lunatic?—should be a question each one of us investigates, reflects on, and ultimately makes a conscious decision about. For according to Jesus, our verdict about him has the most serious consequences for our lives.

And then of course, there is the evidence of the yearning of our hearts. Deep down we all know that our lives are deeply meaningful and important, and we sense that this world, and this earthly, material life, is not all there is. The depth with which we love, our moral sense, and our conscience that tells us our conduct and how we treat people really matters—plus our persistent interest in eternity and life after death—are all signals of transcendence. They are all the natural response of ourselves to the supernatural realities we intuitively know are out there.[12] As the great Christian writer C. S. Lewis put it, "If I find in myself a desire in which no experience in this world can satisfy, the most probable explanation is that I was made for another world."[13]

Yes, God is calling us to himself, and our hearts are restless until they rest in him. God loves each one of us more than we can know. And by his Holy Spirit, and by the sacrificial life and death of Jesus Christ, he has opened a door for us; he has made a way for us to be with him. But we have to be willing to enter through the door he has made. Jesus, and Jesus alone, is that doorway into life everlasting.

There are untold billions all through the last twenty centuries who have found rest in the loving, nurturing, life-giving arms of Jesus. God's grace and mercy is embodied for us in Jesus Christ, and his love for us and his desire to have us know him is always there for us, all of our days.

Mary, these are ideas worth mastering, and worth sharing with others. It is the gospel, it is the power of God that will lead people to salvation (Rom 1:16). I admire the fact you care so much about the people in your life that you want to share these ideas with them. God has placed that desire within you. Keep studying and praying, Mary. God will make a way for you to bring this very good news to those around you.

---

12. On the concept of signals of transcendence see Berger, *Rumor of Angels*.
13. See Lewis, *Mere Christianity*, 120.

SONG TO SAVOR:

"In Christ Alone" by Keith Getty and Stuart Townend, sung by Kristyn Getty.[14]

PRAYER:

"O God, help me to understand the incarnation, and to reflect on Jesus Christ's profound sacrifice for me by becoming a man, and dying in my place. Help me to live a life of gratitude to God the Son who took on human flesh for me to bring me to you, Father. Amen."

MEMORIZE:

> In your relationships with one another, have the same mindset as Christ Jesus: Who, being in very nature God, did not consider equality with God something to be used to his own advantage; rather, he made himself nothing by taking the very nature of a servant, being made in human likeness. And being found in appearance as a man, he humbled himself by becoming obedient to death—even death on a cross! (Phil 2:5–8)

SUGGESTED READING:

Douthat, Ross. *Believe*. Grand Rapids: Zondervan, 2025.
Dreher, Rod. *Living in Wonder: Finding Mystery and Meaning in a Secular Age*. Grand Rapids: Zondervan, 2024.
Markos, Louis. *Apologetics for the Twenty-First Century*. Wheaton, IL: Crossway, 2010.
Moreland, J. P. *Scaling the Secular City*. Grand Rapids: Zondervan, 1987.
Wellum, Stephen J. *God the Son Incarnate*. Wheaton, IL: Crossway, 2016.

---

14. Getty and Getty, "In Christ Alone."

2

Prayer

"I pray because I can't help myself. I pray because I'm helpless. I pray because the need flows out of me all the time, waking and sleeping. It doesn't change God. It changes me."

—C. S. Lewis

"He has infinite attention to spare for each one of us. He does not have to deal with us in the mass. You are as much alone with Him as if you were the only being He had ever created."

—C. S. Lewis

"We say that we believe God to be omniscient; yet a great deal of prayer seems to consist of giving him information."

—C. S. Lewis

From: thebradstetson@gmail.com
To: Teresa

Well, Teresa, I agree with you that prayer is talking to God. That certainly is one type of prayer. I don't know why your friends find the idea so scandalous. After all, God made us in his image to worship him and live with him; it makes sense that he would want us to talk with him, and that he would want to communicate to us, which he does through his word, nature, beauty, the truths of lives, our consciences, our moral sense, and by his Holy Spirit as we pray. He can communicate to us anyway he wants to, of course, but we must always test everything by his word.

The first idea I would like to mention to you about prayer is that it is a practice we should treasure. For Christians accustomed to it, there is simply no feeling as serene and peaceful as bringing concerns to God in prayer, and laying our anxieties and longings before him. I remember one day talking with a Christian leader; let's call him David. He was a man with unique insight and understanding, a well-known Christian author and professor. Our conversation was interrupted by a phone call, which David was expecting. He spoke on the phone for a few minutes about prayer. It seemed as though David and the man who called him were setting up a prayer ministry, or some kind of project that they thought would entail regular, focused prayer.

I remember David recommending to the caller that they recruit people who, he said, "had a sense of ownership" of prayer in their lives. By that, I gather he meant people who think about prayer not as something they do sporadically, or when a need arises, but rather that it is a regular, constant practice for them. David wanted people who would cultivate their prayer life and practice it the way one might practice an instrument each day, developing great facility with it. He wanted people who would become virtuosos of prayer. His understanding was that whatever the kind of prayer—praise, supplication, intercessory, an urgent plea, or any other expression to the Lord—it should become a part of our personal identity, the natural, daily practice and expression of our faith and life.[1]

Let me offer to you, Teresa, just to stimulate your own thinking about prayer, seven principles that I have found helpful.

---

1. For thoughtful discussions of prayer and the Christian life, see, classically, Murray, *With Christ*. See also Keller, *Prayer*; Greig, *How to Pray*; Lewis, *How to Pray*.

Part I: Theological Topics

First, when you pray, be as specific as possible. If you are praying for people, use their names. If you're praying for a situation, try to specify the outcome you are hoping for. Praying for "world peace," while a nice thought, isn't going to work. It's like one man trying to lift a million-pound monolith. Instead, name the world leaders you have in mind, their countries, and something of the challenges they are facing. This specificity is not wise because God otherwise won't know what you mean, but rather it promotes spiritual efficacy. Specificity in prayer serves as a sort of "authorizing" agent. It assists in a human way God bringing about the state of affairs you—and, as a prerequisite, he—both want to see. Think of it as specificity helping to un-jam a logjam, in a spiritual sense. It can help get things moving in the spiritual world.

Second, Teresa, be persistent in prayer. From Rom 12:12 to all throughout the New Testament, we are encouraged to be persistent in prayer. Sometimes it takes a long, long time for something to come to pass. (Remember the story in Daniel chapter 10 about how God's angel was delayed three weeks in responding to Daniel's prayer because of demonic opposition.) Whether we are praying for people or conditions, we have to stay at it; we cannot give up simply because we haven't seen results. The battle is a spiritual one. We may need to pray about how to pray, that is, ask God how we should be praying about a given matter. But pray without ceasing we must (1 Thess 5:17). Visualize a bunch of men holding a huge log and using it as a battering ram against the door of a fortress. The men have to ram the log into the door many times before the door finally gives way. Our experience in prayer can be like that.

I don't want to take any kind of special credit, but I must tell a story about persistence in prayer. Decades ago, very near to my house, there was an abortion center. A "clinic," as it was known. It was busy, and it regularly attracted a lot of attention in the local press because the owner was a wealthy, flamboyant local doctor, and the clinic's manager sometimes had her house picketed by anti-abortion protesters. This was during the abortion culture wars of the 1980s. The location of this abortion business was such that I had to drive by it daily, often more than once, to get home or to just go about town.

So one day as I was driving by it, I thought to myself, instead of just staring at the building and lamenting the horrors happening between its walls, why don't I pray that it will be shut down? At first I thought, that's ridiculous, how could that ever happen, it had already been there for years and it was a profitable business. It had the support of a lot of people in the community. But then I thought, praying it would close couldn't hurt, and besides I was in no hurry; I would be driving by that building every day for years to come.

So, I started praying. Every day as I drove by the killing center, I simply prayed to myself or said in a whisper, "Lord, I pray that evil place would be shut down." I prayed that breath prayer every time I passed by that building, and passing by the building served as a reminder to make my supplication. I had no idea how such a thing could come to pass, or what course of events would have to transpire to bring about its close, but I just prayed that prayer consistently. It was a simple prayer, uttered often and regularly, usually more than once a day, for altogether about eleven years.

Well, about five years went by after I started praying, and the place was still in the news periodically. I noticed the clinic manager's house, which was also near mine, was being steadily upgraded over the months that came and went. A new roof, a newly landscaped front yard, a new garage door. All the regular upgrades a house might have, financed at least in part by her role at the "clinic," the house of horrors. Her increasingly beautiful home served as another reminder to pray, and as a hideous contrast to the ugliness that financed it.

After another couple years, the doctor who owned the clinic started to have troubles with another business he owned in the area, a horse racetrack. I didn't pay much attention, but the problems there started becoming a little more frequent and the press coverage of the racetrack less favorable. Injured horses, unsavory betting, inquiries from the state horse racing commission—the

Part I: Theological Topics

bad publicity started accumulating. I also noticed the protests at the clinic were getting a little larger, and a little better organized.

Then, another few years later, to my astonishment, I read that the doctor who owned the horse track was getting out of that business. It was becoming too stressful, and too expensive. And then, not very long after that, perhaps another couple years or so, as I drove by the killing center one day, I saw a large "For Lease" banner across the front of it! That was it! Suddenly, without notice, the "clinic" was closed!

I was very surprised, in a good way. I was ecstatic. Actually, to tell you the truth, Teresa, I was quite shocked that my prayers had been answered. There was no hint publicly what was happening privately, but obviously, behind the scenes, the prayers of Christians who opposed the presence of this "clinic" were working.

Now, no doubt, many, many Christians far and wide were praying that the killing center be shut down. But this was in the 1980s and into the 1990s, at the height of the American culture wars over abortion, so the man who ran the clinic had a lot of cultural and political support—especially in Southern California, where all this happened. I was never aware of any suggestion that the abortion center might close, and yet, one day it was gone. Now, Teresa, I have no idea what role my little breath prayers uttered through the years played, but it was not nothing. Every prayer we send up to God reaches his ears, and in his perfection he considers them all, and uses them to work as he will.

Third, remember God wants to answer our prayers. When we pray, we have an eager audience in God. He is pleased that we have brought our requests to him, and like a good father he wants to give us what we are asking for. In fact, as Jesus said in Matt 7:11, God, as our heavenly father (not a flawed earthly father), *really* wants to give us good gifts. Now, what we are asking for may not be in our best interests according to his perfect mind, but certainly his strong desire and inclination is to help us and give us what we ask.

Of course, obviously, we shouldn't pray for something illegal or sinful to prevail; obviously God won't answer that prayer. I knew a man once who had his car registration lapse, and he was quite poor and couldn't afford to reregister his car. But he wanted to keep driving, so he forged the registration tags on his license plate, hoping the police wouldn't notice. Well they did, and one day while he was driving they pulled him over. My friend tried to have his misdeed excused by the police. The officer said to him, "Didn't you know that we would notice the tags on your license plate were fake?" My friend answered, "I was praying no police would notice that." The officer chuckled and said, "Why did you pray that God would defend your lie about your car registration?" So, it really is self-evident, isn't it, that God will not be coopted into our schemes.

But still, he is for us, not against us. He wants us to have the desires of our hearts, and he is ready to answer our prayers. And he is that way toward everyone, not just me or you. I had another remarkable experience once that brought that truth home to me.

I was writing and conducting a lot of funerals, working as a funeral chaplain. But the work was, as it always is, rather sporadic. Yet I needed the income, so I prayed with regularity that I would be called for funeral work. And it was remarkable to me that so many times after I prayed, specifically naming various funeral arrangers I knew at different mortuaries, that those very individuals would call me. It was, to my mind, absolutely uncanny. I prayed that, for example, "Mark" at ABC Mortuary would call me for a service, and sure enough, a few days later, "Mark" from that very mortuary would call. Teresa, this happened many, many times over the years. It was amazing. Frankly, I was no doubt puffed up about it. I think I thought—unacknowledged to myself—that I had a special hotline into God's ear.

Well one day I conducted a funeral service in a mortuary chapel, then drove on ahead to the cemetery where the graveside service would take place. I was early, so I was just standing around the grave. Soon after I arrived a woman came whom I knew. She was the "dove lady," a woman who brought birds—they were really pigeons colored white—which would be released during the graveside service. It was called a "dove release," and like me, she depended on funeral arrangers to call her for work. Without any calls to release her doves at a service, she would have no income. So, I was standing there chatting with her, waiting for the people to arrive from the chapel. It was small talk, mostly. I asked her if she'd been very busy, and she said no, not really. Then she said emphatically, "But thank God I got called for this service! I was praying to God that someone would call me so I could have work. I really needed this job. That seems to happen a lot. I cry out to God for help, and then someone calls me for a dove release. That happens all the time."

I looked at her and nodded. I was at once inspired by her faith, and kind of disappointed that I wasn't the only one whose prayers were being answered. I thought I was special. But then I realized, she's special to God too. We both are. He was doing for her exactly what he had been doing for me: hearing our earnest pleas and providing for us. His grace is enough for us, his provision sufficient, and his love impartial. God's amazing love and goodness is for everyone.

Have you ever looked out at a large crowd of people, Teresa, like at a full stadium, and realized that God loves each one of those people equally and totally? He knows each one, everything about them. He knows their thoughts and feelings, hopes and fears. He knows the good things they've done, and the bad things they've done. He knows the tragedies and challenges they will face, and the blessings they will enjoy. He knows them intimately, and loves each one more than we can understand. I remember once seeing a photo of a mass of Chinese people at a rally at Tiananmen Square in Beijing. There must have been about ten thousand people packed together tightly. As I looked at their faces, I couldn't see their individuality, but to God, each individual was fully known and truly loved with a transcendent love beyond human comprehension. There are no anonymous faces to God, and there are no only partially valuable people. No one is intrinsically less than anyone else. Remember when you look out at a sea of faces in a stadium, God loves each individual person as though they were the only person on earth. His infinite attributes and resources and abilities enable him to do that. His unlimited abilities are not stressed by tasks that strike us as difficult.

Fourth, Teresa, prepare by pre-prayer (Phil 4:6–7). This is so important. It is akin to that old Sun-Tzu principle of war: every battle is won before it even starts. If you have a big interview coming up, or if you are going to give some kind of performance, or if you have to have a difficult conversation with someone, prepare by pre-prayer. Pray about the circumstance beforehand. Well ahead of the moment—months, weeks, days—pray that God will give you wisdom and awareness to act appropriately in the moment. Pray that God will give you favor, great favor, with whomever you are going to speak. Pray that God will prepare their hearts and minds to receive favorably what you intend to say to them. God can turn the hearts of men and women any way he wishes. Prevail upon him to act on your behalf in this way. This is not "manifesting" what you want, or in some way trying to create a circumstance by what you say. This is praying to God to accomplish his purposes through you in a way that you are hoping for, consistent with his will for your life. He wants to help you, he wants to give you the good desires of your heart, and he wants you to learn to lean on him for those realities to prevail. He wants us to want him to walk with us through the days and circumstances of our lives.

Fifth, you know, Teresa, God is sovereign over our lives. There are no accidents. Sometimes I am confused by Christians who are accustomed to ascribing circumstances to coincidence. It's not hard for God to bring events and situations about as he prefers. God is an infinite, personal, creative, perfect mind; there are no degrees of difficulty for him. He's not like us. He knows at any instant the number of grains of sand in the world, the exact number of hairs on every human head, and the exact number of houseflies living. This isn't hard for him. He's infinite. Thus, all contingencies of whatever kind are known to him before they happen, or don't.

So I suggest you apply this idea to all the people you have met throughout your life. People you now know, people you have known, and even people you don't yet know but one day will. As you remember them and think of them, pray for them. You can

Part I: Theological Topics

pray for their health; you can pray for problems you know they were having at the time you knew them; pray that God will send people into their lives who will help them draw near to him, and come to know him and love him. It may sound like a trite greeting card slogan, but it's true: God brings people into our lives for a reason. So reflect on who you have known. God brought you to them, and them to you, for a reason. You should pray for them by name. Pray that God will teach you from your experience with them, and pray you will be a positive, godly force in the lives of those around you now, or even in the future.

Now I should hasten to add, Teresa, that there is another critical dimension to our prayer life that we must practice: We must pray for our enemies (Matt 5:44). Of course this is a central teaching of Jesus, but one we conveniently forget. In a world as coarse as ours, where an errant lane change on the freeway could literally bring gunfire upon us, it can be hard to pray for those who oppose us. But we must, and of course such prayers are especially pleasing to God. Anyone can pray for their friends, and people who are nice to them. The spirit of Christ calls us to pray for those who despise us, and wish us ill. This is a sacred duty, and as we fulfill it we will be changed for the better.

Praying for someone toward whom you have held a grudge is a great way to get rid of that grudge and dissolve that destructive anger. If you have hard feelings toward someone, begin to pray for them by name. Ask God to bless their lives, to bring peace and real joy to them, and to bring peace to your relationship with them, as far as it is up to you. As you consistently pray for that person, you will find your hard feelings toward them dissolve away. Your heart will be softened, and you will be emancipated from the harmful and ugly feelings that define a grudge, and so much of the spirit of our time.

I'll never forget my experience with a neighbor of mine. Let's call him "Jim." He lived right next to me, and he had a large, expansive backyard. And the layout of his backyard was such that his pool and patio, and his entertainment center, were all tucked into the very corner of his yard that was closest to my office, where I spent a lot of time. The walls and windows of my office were thin, and his activities and music were loud. He had worked in construction when he was a younger man, so he had a lot of construction equipment, and he loved using it. In particular, he had a hydraulic jackhammer. It was a gigantic device that road crews used to demolish asphalt and pavement. Well, Jim was fond of periodically removing the concrete in his backyard with this contraption, and then pouring new concrete in a different kind of design. Then, six months or a year later, he would repeat the days-long exercise. The noise—not to mention the vibration in my office—was substantial.

Well, one early Saturday morning, while yet another demolition was in progress, I got upset. I quickly walked over to Jim's house and found him inside his open garage while the work crew was in the backyard going at it. I told him the noise was too loud and too frequent. I was particularly angry that morning as my daughter had been sick with the flu, and she called out to me that the noise had awakened her. I scolded Jim and told him how upset I was. He was unmoved by my displeasure. He said he at least he was trying to improve his yard, and that mine was a disgrace. He called me a nasty name, and said I should lose weight. Then he opened up his garage refrigerator and tossed me a Diet Coke, saying, "You should drink this." I left in a huff.

Well, the same patterns of construction noise continued for a few more years. Then, a new neighbor—Jack—moved in on the other side of me, and Jack befriended Jim. He started to tell me a bit about Jim's life and family. He spoke fondly of Jim. I started to see Jim more as a person and not simply as an annoying neighbor. Then one day Jack told me that Jim had stage four colon cancer.

I finally realized I should be praying for Jim, and that I should have reached out to him years ago and befriended him. So I began praying for his healing from cancer, and for some of the other problems I had heard of through Jack. A couple years went by, and I continued to pray for Jim. I noticed that my hard feelings toward him were being replaced by my prayers for him. When I would drive by his house, instead of thinking about how annoying he was, I'd whisper a prayer for his recovery. I started to care about

Part I: Theological Topics

him. Another two years went by, and Jack told me how hard Jim was fighting cancer, and how his doctors and family thought he was valiant and courageous. Jim had undergone nearly 130 rounds of chemotherapy. I kept praying for Jim, and my anger at him became a feeling of the past. I didn't feel mad at him, but rather I felt an admiration, because I knew he was fighting to live. He had a wife and two kids—and a lot of friends—and he didn't want to die.

Well, another year later Jack told me Jim was near death. He was on hospice. One day, I noticed a bunch of unfamiliar cars at his house, and it seemed like a death vigil. A few days later I heard Jim had died. I thought about how brave he had been, and I felt guilt and remorse at the course our non-relationship had taken. I felt a true disappointment at his passing. Prayer for him had taken me from hostility to sympathy to admiration.

Well, Teresa, I hope that story reminds you to pray all the time, in every circumstance, and to reach out to those around you. Prayer is the best medicine known to human beings, I think. It's therapeutic for the person praying, and it's often a great benefit to the person being prayed for. Prayer will reduce anxiety, hate, contempt, distrust, and lack of self-confidence, and it will replace destructive, harsh feelings with authentic and lasting empathy and peace.[2]

Sixth and lastly, Teresa, I want to say a word about praying for the dead. Of course when someone we love dies we don't let go of them; we still love them and feel a great sense of continuing attachment to them, so it's natural for us to want to pray to God about them. Now, when a believer dies and is with God, they are living in God's heavenly kingdom, and they are no longer in lack. So we don't need to pray that they will be cared for or safe, because the Lord of life is already seeing to that in a manner that is so profoundly wonderful it surpasses what we can even begin to ask or imagine.

But we can pray—for anyone who has passed away—that God will be glorified in their being. We can pray that God will be

---

2. For a helpful discussion along these lines, see Matthews and Clark, *Faith Factor*; Tolson and Koenig, *Healing Power of Prayer*.

glorified in their legacy in this world, and that their memory will be a blessing to all who have known them. We can pray that God will continue to teach us from their lives, and that we will honor their memory in our own lives. A person's life is like a book, and when we knew and loved them in this life, you might say we read every page. But the story of their life doesn't end when their body dies. Their story continues on, and we will continue to write their story, as it were, with our memories of them. And we can pray that God will give us new insights and understandings of them and our time with them, even after their bodies have died. The Holy Spirit can bring all kinds of comfort and lessons to us as we reflect on our loved one's life, and all of our experiences and conversations with them, great and small. There is something to learn in every circumstance, even in the passing of someone we love very much. So we should pray that God would give us new insight and knowledge from the lives of people we have known, because that awareness will enhance our lives and help us to contribute to the humanity of others, enhancing their lives in turn.

Well, Teresa, I admire your praying heart. I think God has placed this calling on your life. It is a gift. Never tire of going within your heart, and from there reaching out to God on behalf of people and a world that needs him more than they usually know. Memorize Rom 12:12: "Be joyful in hope, patient in affliction, faithful in prayer."

SONG TO SAVOR:

"Still" by Reuben Morgan, sung by Natashia Midori.[3]

PRAYER:

> This, then, is how you should pray: "Our Father in heaven, hallowed be your name, your kingdom come, your will be done, on earth as it is in heaven. Give us today our daily bread. And forgive us our debts, as we also have

3. Midori, "Still."

forgiven our debtors. And lead us not into temptation, but deliver us from the evil one." (Matt 6:9–13)

MEMORIZE:

And when you pray, do not be like the hypocrites, for they love to pray standing in the synagogues and on the street corners to be seen by others. Truly I tell you, they have received their reward in full. But when you pray, go into your room, close the door and pray to your Father, who is unseen. Then your Father, who sees what is done in secret, will reward you. And when you pray, do not keep on babbling like pagans, for they think they will be heard because of their many words. Do not be like them, for your Father knows what you need before you ask him. (Matt 6:5–8)

SUGGESTED READING:

Greig, Pete. *How to Pray: A Simple Guide for Normal People.* Colorado Springs, CO: NavPress, 2019.

Keller, Timothy. *Prayer: Experiencing Awe and Intimacy with God.* New York: Penguin, 2016.

MacArthur, John. *Alone With God: Rediscovering the Power and Passion of Prayer.* Colorado Springs, CO: David C. Cook, 2011.

Packer, J. I., and Carolyn Nystrom. *Prayer: Finding Our Way Through Duty to Delight.* Downers Grove, IL: InterVarsity, 2009.

Willard, Dallas. *Hearing God: Developing a Conversational Relationship with God.* Downers Grove, IL: InterVarsity, 2012.

3
Hypocrisy

"Christianity is a good idea, someone should try it."
—Mark Twain

"This year, or this month, or, more likely, this very day, we have failed to practice ourselves the kind of behavior we expect from other people."
—C. S. Lewis

"Of all bad men religious bad men are the worst."
—C. S. Lewis

From: thebradstetson@gmail.com
To: Ted

Thanks for your thoughtful question, Ted. Yes, hypocrisy is something you are right to hate, and to strive to avoid. But I've got some bad news: you're still going to be a hypocrite. You will fall short of the ideals you know you ought to uphold as a Christian. But that's par for the course, so to speak. Read the first chapter of 1 John; the apostle reassures believers that their sins are covered by Jesus Christ our advocate.

Part I: Theological Topics

But let's dig deeper into this problem, because I think there is a lot of confusion about hypocrisy. First of all, doing what you know to be right, even if you don't feel enthusiastic about it, is not hypocrisy. For example, going to church even though you may not feel like going is not hypocrisy. Forsaking vengeance when you feel tempted to take vengeance is not hypocrisy. Doing what is right in any given context, even though you do it out of a sense of duty rather than an excited enthusiasm, is not hypocrisy. To the contrary, this is more like moral virtue and maturity. You don't have to derive an emotional charge out of doing what is good in order to do it. In fact, so often we don't feel an emotional pull towards doing our duty.

I'm reminded of an observation once made by the great French Christian philosopher Simone Weil. She said something to the effect that imaginary evil is alluring, fascinating, and exciting to contemplate. But actual evil is boring, drudgery, and monotonous. Conversely, imaginary goodness is boring, tiresome, and uninteresting. But actual goodness is exhilarating, enlivening, and thrillingly uplifting. This is a great insight, and reflection on it will help us understand our own natures, and our own disinclination toward the good. You know, Ted, Jesus died for a reason: We need a Savior. We are not just fine the way we naturally are. We are fallen and sinful, and prone to continue in it. That is our set inclination. We are totally unable to save ourselves.[1]

Weil's observation about the thrill of goodness was brought home to me recently. I was taking some old clothes to a Goodwill drop-off station near my house. I had a couple of boxes of stuff, and it was going to only take a moment. I pulled up to the drop-off station, and a young woman, about age twenty-five, approached my car to help me deposit my donation. She was a bit overweight and disheveled, with long brown hair that hung down over her forehead. She moved slowly, and her expression and body language were glum. I got out of my car and opened my back door where the boxes were, and I handed one to her and said "Thank you."

---

1. For sound discussion, see Demarest, *Cross and Salvation*; Trueman, *Grace Alone*.

She took it and then returned. The second box was a bit heavier, and I apologized to her. I said I couldn't pick it up because I had two hernias, and it was sort of heavy. She reached in and got it no problem, and carried it away. She then brought my donation receipt and handed it to me. I took it and said perfunctorily, "OK thanks, take care." She stood still, looked at me and said, "Thank you for being so nice to me."

I was taken aback. I had been really only minimally polite, but obviously, apparently, working at the Goodwill drop-off site, she had been accustomed to harsh treatment (no doubt by many Christians). I thanked her again and drove off, but I remember feeling both sorry for her and also excited that she regarded my conduct as kind. Quite by accident, I had acted rightly towards this suffering soul, and I felt a kind of exhilaration at that realization. The thrill of goodness in human action is real, and though it is hard to imagine and anticipate, it far outweighs the fleeting and superficial pleasure of wrongdoing.

So Weil's observation is important as a motivational insight for behaving well. But we must also develop within ourselves a real hatred of personal hypocrisy—our hypocrisy. We must cultivate our meta-desires, that is, what we desire to desire. We have to want to want to honor God, and want to not want to dishonor him. We must desire to live lives of integrity in Christ, so much so that hypocrisy becomes revolting to us. Try to think of a time you learned of another Christian's hypocrisy, and how you felt upon finding out about it. You probably had that sinking "oh no" feeling that comes when you see someone embarrass themselves in some way. We should have the feeling that says, "I don't want to be that guy."

I remember first hearing about Ravi Zacharias' hypocrisy. He was a brilliant Christian apologist who traveled the world, preaching the gospel and defending Christian truth claims all over media and universities. He was a great Christian leader. Shortly after his death in 2020, it became widely known that he had for years engaged in unethical behavior with women, and it was a source of shame to his organization, and of course to his reputation. It became apparent that he had acted improperly for a long time, in violation of his Christian calling and witness. The gap between who he claimed to be and how he acted was substantial, and hypocritical. This distressing epitaph to his life eclipsed the message of so much of his work.[2]

We should strive to live our lives before an audience of one (God). It is he who we seek to impress, not mere men. As we mature in Christ, the gap between who we claim to be and who we actually are should get smaller and smaller. We claim to be followers of Christ, so our conduct should look like his.

And as Christians of course, whether we're famous or not, the spotlight is upon us, even if only among our circle of friends and family. So often non-Christians monitor our conduct on the hunt to find our shortcomings or failings, thinking that if they see us fail or be a hypocrite that this therefore excuses them from the claims of the gospel. Yet, they are not made innocent by our guilt; they are not absolved of their wrongdoing because of our hypocrisy. After all, if I am a liar or a cheater but I affirm that two plus two equals four, the math is not proven wrong by my bad character. A truth claim is true or false on its own merits; it is not made true or false by the good or bad character of the person making the truth claim. Christianity is true, even if individual Christians are poor representatives of that truth.

So the hypocrisy of Christians does not nullify the truth of the gospel, nor, in truth, does it prevent those God has called to himself to answer that call. God is well able to draw unto himself those whom he will, however morally clumsy and hypocritical professing Christians are.

And yet, as individual Christians, we have to ask ourselves, "Are we doing all we can possibly do to live the gospel, to honor God in our lives?" Remember, grace is opposed to earning, not effort, and in these times it seems so many Christians are merely living a gospel of "sin maintenance." That is, we are living on a treadmill of conduct that is only vaguely Christian, with a heavy, heavy dose of contemporary popular culture flavoring our character. We have to

---

2. For insightful discussion of Ravi Zacharias' hypocrisy, see Hansen, "Ravi Zacharias."

transcend the gospel of sin maintenance and enter into a second-by-second, minute-by-minute, hour-by-hour, walking fellowship with God. This is what it means to live a life of integrity in Christ, and yes, you can bet if you do it you will seem a bit odd to those around you. Which is, of course, as it should be. Ted, if you aren't regarded as a bit strange by those around you who are nonbelievers or nominal believers, then you're doing something wrong, or, I should say, not enough right. I knew a man who used to say, whenever someone he knew from the past became a Christian, that so-and-so "went Jesus on us." That was his way of dismissing the born-again experience that an old friend of his had, and their new pattern of conduct, whenever it happened. Well, without being harsh or insensitive to those around us, may it be said of us all that we "went Jesus." We would do well to ask ourselves if those around us—based on our conduct—think that Jesus is indeed the center of our life like that.

I recall I once did a funeral for a man—call him "Bill"—who had led an excellent life. His wife and kids and grandkids loved him deeply. He had a lot of friends, and had accomplished a lot. It was a great life. He was a witty guy, and had a lot of signature sayings he used throughout the years. He was fond of saying to people, "If you could ask God one question right now, what would it be?" Before someone could respond, Bill would interject, "I'd ask him, 'How am I doing?'" I think it would be wise of each of us, in a quiet and introspective moment, to ask God that very question.

Lastly, Ted, though as I've said hypocrisy is a condition we must hate, there is a very real sense in which hypocrisy has gotten a bad rap. Hypocrisy hasn't gotten the respect it deserves. Let me explain.

The old saying "Hypocrisy is the tribute vice pays to virtue" captures an important truth. Pretending to be virtuous when you are not tacitly admits virtue is preferable to vice. The hypocrite in his pose is in fact pointing to the moral necessity of virtue.

And which is better, anyway, to do wrong and say it's right, or to do wrong and forthrightly admit it's wrong? The latter is better. When we sin and fall short of who we know we should be, we must admit that to God and ask for his forgiveness, and for him to give us repentance. This is a part of the formula for moral and spiritual growth. When we act hypocritically and wrongly as Christians, we must acknowledge that, and not try to justify it in any way. Obedience in the first place is the best course for us to take, but as a matter of fact every Christian—sooner or later, more so or less so—fails at that. Our sins and our own hypocrisy can be pretty subtle, but we can be sure they are there, even if we don't always see them. After all, we are very good at convincing ourselves that we aren't that bad. Which is why we like to see other people, particularly other Christians, fail and fall. It makes us look good by comparison, or so we think. Christian *schadenfreude* is a real problem, spiritually corrupting, and we should be on guard against it.

Well, this trick of mental gymnastics doesn't fool God; he knows all about us, and what we have done. Though we can deceive ourselves about our own virtue, we are utterly naked before him.

Now, the practice of hypocrisy for Christians can become rather wearying and discouraging. Some Christians, after repeated moral failings and the shame they feel at their own hypocrisy, become discouraged and turn away from asking God's forgiveness. They may think that because they have asked God to forgive them five hundred times for the same sin that he won't forgive them again, or that the whole Christian project is pointless for them.

These are terrible mistakes of judgment. Ted: God will not tire of forgiving you, and he will never give up on you. He will never stop loving you, and he will never stop forgiving you when you come to him. He will never turn you away. Ceasing to ask God to forgive us for repeated sins is actually a kind of projection or anthropomorphism. It's a case of thinking God is like a human being. When people wrong us repeatedly we well might give up on them. But God understands us; he understands what it is to be a human being, and he can teach us to grow in our faith, and he can train us in righteousness. He does this by his grace; he changes us through his mercy. If we are willing and wanting to follow him more than our own preferences, he will deliver us into the long obedience in the same direction that is genuine discipleship. And therein is the only path for human fulfillment and happiness. Remember the saying so true: "No Jesus, No Peace; Know Jesus, Know Peace."

So cultivate those meta-desires, Ted, and see yourself honoring God. You want to please him, and you want to want to please him. You don't want to displease him, and you want to not want to be willing to displease him. Reflect on that.

You know, there's one more aspect of hypocrisy that I think is overlooked. It's along the lines of the old "fake it 'til you make it" slogan. C. S. Lewis once noted that we eventually become what we are pretending to be. By pretending to be a mature Christian who honors God, even when we believe that we are not that, we make progress towards becoming the virtuous believer we are pretending to be. God will continually draw us closer to him as we yearn for him and long to please him. Never give up, Ted, seeking to honor God. Live as you would if you were really living a life of integrity in Christ, and, in time, you actually will be. Remember what Jesus said at the end of Matthew's Gospel: "I am with you always" (Matt 28:20).

SONG TO SAVOR:

"Create in Me a Clean Heart" by Keith Green.[3]

PRAYER:

O God, forgive my iniquity, though it is great. Empower me by your Holy Spirit to honor you in all things, and to live a life of integrity in Christ. Make me single-minded, Lord, and lead me and guide me in your way. Work your will in my life, O God, and equip me with everything good for doing your will. Draw me ever closer to you, O Lord. Amen.

---

3. Green, "Create in Me."

Part I: Theological Topics

MEMORIZE:

And do this, understanding the present time: The hour has already come for you to wake up from your slumber, because our salvation is nearer now than when we first believed. The night is nearly over; the day is almost here. So let us put aside the deeds of darkness and put on the armor of light. Let us behave decently, as in the daytime, not in carousing and drunkenness, not in sexual immorality and debauchery, not in dissension and jealousy. Rather, clothe yourselves with the Lord Jesus Christ, and do not think about how to gratify the desires of the flesh. (Rom 13:11–14)

SUGGESTED READING:

Lowery, David. *Following Jesus in an Age of Hypocrisy*. Eugene, OR: Wipf & Stock, 2020.

Lutzer, Erwin. *The Power of a Clear Conscience: Let God Free You from Your Past*. Eugene, OR: Harvest House, 2016.

Reeves, Michael. *Evangelical Pharisees: The Gospel as Cure for the Church's Hypocrisy*. Wheaton, IL: Crossway, 2023.

Ten Elshof, Gregg. *I Told Me So: Self-Deception and the Christian Life*. Grand Rapids: Eerdmans, 2009.

Willard, Dallas. *Renovation of the Heart*. Colorado Springs, CO: NavPress, 2002.

4
Evangelism

"What we practise, not (save at rare intervals) what we preach, is usually our great contribution to the conversion of others."

—C. S. Lewis

"My feeling about people in whose conversion I have been allowed to play a part is always mixed with awe and even fear: such as a boy might feel on first being allowed to fire a rifle. The disproportion between his puny finger on the trigger and the thunder and lightning which follow is alarming. And the seriousness with which the other party takes my words always raises the doubt whether I have taken them seriously enough myself."

—C. S. Lewis

"I believe in Christianity as I believe that the sun has risen—not only because I see it, but because by it I see everything else."

—C. S. Lewis

Part I: Theological Topics

From: thebradstetson@gmail.com
To: Tim

Thanks for writing, Tim. I don't know why the PowerPoint didn't work, but I'm glad you could hear me, despite the malfunctioning microphone. Yes, I do have a loud voice. There's a story to that, believe it or not.

For all my life, up until age thirty-three, my speaking voice was normal. But when I was thirty-three, I was diagnosed with an acoustic neuroma brain tumor. That's a benign tumor that grows on the hearing nerve, right where the hearing nerve connects to the brain. While the tumor is always benign, it's still life-threatening and has to be removed. Usually, though not always, you lose your hearing when they remove the tumor. That's what happened to me. So, since September of 1996, I've been 100 percent deaf in my left ear. I won't bore you with the many adjustments I've had to make, and am still making, but suffice to say it's a big life change to endure.

One of the realities of my hearing loss is that I naturally adjusted the volume of my speaking voice upward, so I still sounded normal to myself instead of muffled and distant. After all, my brain now heard only half of what it used to hear. So if I speak in a normal voice now—which I do if people tell me stop yelling at them—I can hardly hear myself.

Now, all of that happened in 1996. At that time and for the next decade to follow, one of my writing interests was grief and bereavement. Writing on those topics led me to want to help grieving people. Gradually, I started to develop a desire to write and conduct funerals and memorial services. Eventually, I did my first one in August of 2008. Those services are often outside, and whether they take place inside a chapel, some other room, or outside, many of the attendees are often elderly and hard of hearing.

So, having a strong voice allowing me to talk over the ambient noise outside at a cemetery (caused by trucks or cars, lawn mowers, overhead jets), or loud enough for hearing impaired old folks to hear me, has turned out to be a blessing. I can't tell you how many times an attendee at one of these services came up to me afterward and thanked me for using a loud voice, and complained that usually they can't hear what the speaker at such a service is saying.

A divine paradox indeed. When I had the brain tumor in 1996, I had no intention of officiating at funerals. But in time, the loss I experienced became in part a benefit to me. Our losses of all kinds can be like that, sometimes. What seems pointless to us, and all and only bad, later becomes a part of us that is helpful to others, and a way that God uses us to help others, and to even bring a new and different kind of fulfillment to our own lives. I'll bet you can think of an event or an experience in your own life where what was a disappointment and a source of pain later became something that was a positive help to you or others, even though it still hurt. I think God is good at not wasting our experiences, even the hard ones. There is something you can learn in every circumstance.

Anyway, Tim, I digress. You wrote to me explaining that you felt frustrated at not being able to communicate about your faith. You said that all your friends, most of whom aren't Christians, think your faith is silly or childish, and intellectually unserious. And you also said that when you actually talk about the gospel, the words don't come easily, and you feel like you aren't describing Christian beliefs or ideas clearly.

Well, first, Tim, let me say that your questions are good ones, and common. Yes, young or old, a lot of Christians feel as you do. They're frustrated at the contempt with which their beliefs are met, and they wish they gave better answers when describing their faith.

Though there are complex reasons for the cultural contempt for Christianity, and though there are comprehensive and detailed answers you can give to vindicate your faith in the minds of reasonable and fair-minded people, I actually think there is a simple, single answer to both your questions. It is this: Simply live your Christian faith authentically and holistically. That is, live a life of integrity in Christ. Do your best to honor him in all you do (which starts by praying to him to empower you to do just that). Live the gospel, and you will find that the Holy Spirit uses your life to speak

Part I: Theological Topics

to others' hearts about the love of God. A Christian life humbly, truly lived is the most eloquent testimony and apologetic you could ever possibly give. In fact, your life and your story is a far more powerful argument for Christ than any rational, evidential, or philosophical explanation. People connect to the personal, and they connect to stories.

Now, I'm all for studying apologetics, and as Peter says in 1 Pet 3:16, "Always be prepared to give an answer to everyone who asks you to give the reason for the hope that you have. Do this with gentleness and respect." But, note, the first part of that same verse says, "In your hearts revere Christ as Lord." So Scripture itself specifies that our words about our faith should be set within the context of a personal piety, a personal commitment to a life of true discipleship to Jesus. Our lives are really to be an "existential witness," the power of which God himself will make clear to those around you.

Remember, Tim, the truth is that people who reject the gospel don't do so for intellectual reasons, even though they may claim they do. The real, deeper reasons are psychological, emotional, familial, and spiritual. Their hearts are darkened, and their wills are not inclined to embrace Jesus as Lord. Now, this human reality is cause for compassion on our part towards nonbelievers, not anger or contempt. Maybe they have had experience with hypocritical Christians, and on that basis felt alienated from the gospel. Maybe they have personal habits or addictions that they know they would have to give up if they committed themselves to Christ. Maybe they have imbibed the toxic liquid of contemporary culture that urges people to "be their own master" and "celebrate themselves" or "be the best version of themselves they can be." It's all nonsense. All those reasons for rejecting Jesus are mistaken inferences on the part of the nonbeliever who had those experiences and was exposed to those ideas. Yet, people often think like that.

So the best apologetic you can give—and your calling as a Christian anyway—is to live your faith. Your character is the greatest and most significant piece of evidence you can offer other people. Now remember, your Christian faith is God's work in you, it's not an accomplishment of your will. But, also remember, grace is opposed to earning, not to effort. You can take positive steps every moment, hour, and day to grow in Christ, and to develop an outlook on the challenges of life that is like his.

How to do that? Well, that's the story of Matthew, Mark, Luke, and John. That's the message of all of the New Testament, and the Old Testament. It the testimony of great Christians through the centuries; it is the story of the church universal. There are great Christians the world over, Tim; strive to be worthy to be among them. Keep studying, keep reading, keep growing. And, keep doing. You need to do charity and acts of service to others, as we are called to do. Remember, Tim, obedience brings understanding, and your faith needs to breathe by doing good (without telling other people about it). Through reading, prayer, worship, and Bible study, we inhale, and through serving others with our deeds we exhale. This is how our faith breathes and grows.

From: thebradstetson@gmail.com
To: Tim

Hi Tim, thanks for emailing again. I appreciate your passion! I admire your desire to really reach your peers with God's love for them in Christ. I think you do have the gift of evangelism, and you are quite right, I think, that in every culture and in every time the evangelist is called to preach Christ and him crucified in a manner most fluent with prevailing cultural winds, without being tossed or controlled by them. We want to speak the language of our social setting, without accommodating the timeless gospel message to the assumptions, values, and idols of our time. That's easier said than done, but that is the Christian's calling.

I understand your frustration at feeling as though you're swimming upstream to get a fair hearing for your Christian views. But I would suggest that you not focus on that too much. Don't let yourself slip into a victim mentality. Remember, the God of the universe is not disadvantaged or hindered by a culture (or social structures, or individuals) set against him. He knows how to accomplish his will.

Every age and culture in which Christians live has its own challenges for believers who know they must bear witness, in character, deed, and word, to the truth of the birth, ministry, death, resurrection, and return of Jesus Christ.[1]

As such challenges go, American Christians living in the 2020s and 2030s have it remarkably easy. Yes, there are the cultural slights, double standards, insults, and erosions of religious liberty, but throughout history—and still in many places today—the hardships some Christians face are not the constraint of their religious expressions, but the constriction of their very throats. Christians are still murdered, all over the globe, for naming the name of Christ. Anti-Christian persecution is rampant in North Korea, Pakistan, Somalia, Nigeria, and elsewhere in Africa, for example. Just yesterday, I read of a Palestinian Christian, a man who had just come to faith in Christ, who, while away from his family on a trip, was murdered by Islamists. They cut his body into fourths and mailed the pieces back to the man's family as a warning to them and the community not to convert to Christianity. Such episodes should remind us that the word "persecution"—which Evangelicals here are sometimes wont to use to lament their cultural disenfranchisement—has an altogether different meaning for Christians elsewhere.

So what then are Evangelical Christians to do, here and now, as they seek to reach out with the love of Jesus Christ? I would like to suggest to you ten vital ideas that must be kept in the front of our minds.

First, as an awareness of what other Christians in other places face suggests, we should embrace and cultivate a deep sense of gratitude regarding all of life. In other words, we must count our blessings, and name them one by one, in the words of the old

---

1. Portions of this discussion are taken from *The Truth About Tolerance* by Brad Stetson and Joseph G. Conti. Copyright (c) 2005 by Brad Stetson and Joseph G. Conti. Used by permission of InterVarsity Press, P. O. Box 1400, Downers Grove, IL 60515, USA. www.ivpress.com.

spiritual. It is not enough to simply render to God in prayer a general, all-encompassing "thank you" for our blessings. Rather, we should comprehensively reflect, and specifically name to God—and one another, when appropriate—the realities, relationships, circumstances, and commodities for which we are thankful. From his provision for our salvation and relationship with him; to our friends and families; to opportunities for school and work; to food, clothing, shelter, and luxuries; to hardships and sufferings, we could probably spend quite a long time just in thanksgiving over the details of our lives. As we do this as a regular practice, we develop a deep consciousness of gratitude, a self-pervading awareness of God's hand continually at work in our lives. A personal orientation of habitual gratitude to God brings peace to our lives, and a settled confidence that will help us minister to others, including evangelistically.

Inasmuch as we live in an age of ingratitude, where the will to power is exalted as somehow noble and indicative of strength, the warm, sweet aroma of a grateful heart will stand out to people, and in itself speak to them of a better way. And of course, a personal disposition of thankfulness sharpens the mind, helping us to understand all manner of things as they really are.

And I would hasten to add, we would do well to also realize that our lives now, where we are in the continuum of history, is not accidental. God has placed us where we are, and when we are, for his reasons. Your placement as a Christian in the twenty-first century living where you do is not merely an accident or coincidence. God in his wise providence has chosen you for this time and place. You have gifts and abilities and potentials that are just right for your time, and he is ready to use you now. Be grateful for that, too, Tim. You have something unique and helpful to offer to everyone in your life.

A second principle we must remind ourselves of regularly is that moral excellence must be a reality in our lives. This is not to deny our need for God's grace, or the enduring reality of our fallenness, but as a spate of writers in the area of spiritual formation have recently reminded us, we can train in righteousness.[2] Honoring God in our lives does not happen by accident. We can and must plan for it, and practice or "work out" with the spiritual disciplines until we are formed in Christ, a process never truly over for us on this earth, even in the most advanced disciples of Jesus. You can be sure that the non-Christians in your life who know of your faith are watching you, to see instances of hypocrisy and moral failing. They feel, perhaps subconsciously, that they are excused from the claims of Christ if you fail. Or, perhaps they think that the gospel is somehow disproved or invalidated by your poor character. Such is not the case, as I've said, but human beings are skilled at making excuses for their own persistence in rejecting God. The deep truth in this tension that every Christian has with those around him, though, is that the nonbelievers in your life are, in their heart of hearts, secretly hoping you will show them a better way. They want you to show them the heart of Christ, because there is within them, too, a subtle yearning to know their Creator, and to be made right with him. Through moral excellence and true compassion in our own character, we can help create an interpersonal and social environment which inclines the ears of those around us to the voice of God's Spirit, speaking to them in those still, silent moments, when the mirror of the soul is clear and un-fogged by the day's hectic business.

Thirdly, a strong ingredient in the churning soul of the unregenerate person is a commitment to self-justification. It is as though self-justification is the "default" position of the human soul. We find it easy to convince ourselves we are not so bad, we can figure things out, we can take care of ourselves, and we don't need a Savior. For Americans today, who value independence, are probably self-sufficient if not affluent in their own lives, and have been exposed to basic themes of Christianity through American culture—their cultural acquaintance serving as a kind of inoculation against genuine Christianity—the penchant for self-justification is especially strong. This shell can be hard to pierce; but knowing it is

---

2. For example, Willard, *Divine Conspiracy*, and Wiilard, *Spirit of the Disciplines*.

there and knowing its composition is helpful in understanding the psychology of the non-Christian.

Self-justification as a psycho-emotional, intellectual, and spiritual quality manifests itself in many ways, including various New Age eccentricities (recall G. K. Chesterton's quip along the lines that when people stop believing in God they don't believe in nothing, they believe in anything), an essentially religious devotion to politics, a workaholic pursuit of career advancement, and moral relativism. This latter endeavor is an exercise in psychological self-protection. If there are no objective moral duties, the relativist subconsciously reasons, then nothing I do can be wrong, therefore nothing is wrong with me. Moral relativism is a specious way of acquitting oneself at the bar of conscience. Our natural moral sense and the Holy Spirit tell us we fall short of the good, but rather than accept that about ourselves, and hopefully find our way to the foot of the cross in repentance, we rationalize our misbehavior. Indeed, E. Michael Jones in *Degenerate Moderns* has perceptively described much of the intellectual edifice of modernity—through studying the lives and thought of Freud, Margaret Mead, Alfred Kinsey, and other prophets of contemporary secularism—as self-justification for sexual misbehavior specifically.[3] The relativist pull in this context is especially strong to people, because it allows them to continue practicing or pursuing sexual activities the Judeo-Christian ethic regards as morally wrong. Relativism licenses them, in their minds, to say it is the Judeo-Christian ethic which is wrong and unreasonable, not their particular sexual predilection.

A psychological self-deceit very similar to this takes place regarding tolerance, and it helps explain our contemporary confusion over the idea. If I manifest a total tolerance (that is, no standards of behavior) toward others, then I cannot be a hypocrite regarding my own failings, since I made no judgments about others. In other words, by redefining tolerance as affirmation of others' behavioral choices, whatever they may be, in my mind I loose myself from any moral standards of conduct that I may fail to keep. So it psychologically pays not to judge others, because then I don't

3. Jones, *Degenerate Moderns*.

have to judge myself, or accept the legitimacy of someone else's judgment of me.

Although this mechanism enjoys widespread use in the minds of contemporary Americans, it is patently childish, I think, for three reasons. First, my wrongdoing is not made right simply by the fact that I'm not the only one who does it (whatever "it" is). Second, this psychological self-deceit is just a way of trying to fake out our own conscience. It is a hopeless flight. Our awareness of our wrongdoing stays with us, even if we deny we have done wrong. Our moral sense is hardwired into our consciousness; we cannot truly get rid of it. Deep down, even the worst tyrant, sadist, or sociopath knows he is practicing wrongdoing. Even the seared conscience is not completely, absolutely dead. It is powerless, but not nonexistent. Third, judging oneself—or accepting reasonable criticisms of oneself from others—is not an activity that should be avoided. It is no less than the path to moral progress and character development. Of course we should admit to ourselves our genuine wrongdoing, and of course we should, in sensitive, wise, and patient ways, appropriately offer constructive criticism to those we care about regarding their own ethical shortcomings. That is proper compassion. Ignoring problems that need to be fixed is not a very effective method of caretaking, either for our own souls, the souls of others, or indeed anything we truly care about.

A fourth idea we must keep before us as we think about evangelism is the fundamentally angry character of contemporary life. Many, many people, it seems, go through their daily lives with a supply of rage strapped to their backs, like a deep-sea diver might have three large oxygen tanks tied to his back. This supply of rage, always at the ready, might be unleashed at the slightest provocation: a long red light, a pedestrian in the crosswalk in front of us, being put on hold when calling the pharmacy, a glare from a stranger on the street, a long checkout line at the supermarket. The particular circumstance that brings to the surface the swirling brew of rage that lies below appearances is irrelevant. The problem people face in embracing the gospel message and that Christians face in communicating it is circumventing this roadblock of rage.

For people must face the question, if even subconsciously, "Who would I be without this fury that is a part of me?" People live with anger every moment of every day, like a malevolent Siamese twin, and it becomes an integral part of their self-understanding. Many people wrongly understand anger as empowering, and its expression as a demonstration of strength. Thus they think to leave their anger is to become weak and vulnerable. This is an objectively false sentiment, but given the character of contemporary life it is understandable why those long joined with anger might feel this way. The believer must find a way, first through personal example, to show others that true strength lies in rest, not rage; peace, not petulance; hope, not hate; and patience, not pride.

Fifth, Tim, we must remember that deeds, not words, are the most effective tools for evangelism. The old saying "I can't hear your words, because your deeds are speaking too loudly" illustrates the natural human revulsion we feel when people hypocritically tell us to believe or do one thing, then they themselves act contrary to what they have just prescribed for us. It is a simple but important truth of human psychology that one must earn the right to a serious hearing from people when the topic is serious. The preaching of the cross impacts people much more deeply when you have shown them in deed that you care for them. If you show someone you care about them as a human being, that their wellbeing matters to you, and you demonstrate in your conduct before them your own unconditional commitment in Christ, then your words of witness will naturally be weighty to their ears. Be nice to people, and they'll probably listen to what you have to say. God can use what you say to work in their heart and mind much more effectively if you, as an ambassador of Christ, have well represented your Master.

How then do we go about developing within ourselves true and genuine concern for the acquaintance or colleague or neighbor God has brought into our lives? The first and most primary means is by praying for them. With a specific, sustained, focused practice of prayer regarding a particular person, God will develop within us an authentic concern for that person. We will start to

PART I: THEOLOGICAL TOPICS

care about their life and circumstances. This real sense of connection to them will naturally lead to acts of civility, kindness, and service that make it clear to them that you are a person of integrity, and this is a naturally attractive quality to people today, who live in an age of hype, hypocrisy, spin, and image.

Sixth, Christian apologists must remember that overwhelmingly—as I noted earlier—people in contemporary American society reject the gospel for spiritual, psychological, and emotional reasons, not for intellectual ones. Few non-Christians have conducted any kind of systematic, comprehensive review of the historical, textual, philosophical or psychological evidences for the truth of Christianity. There are internal, nonrational barriers to Christian commitment, always ultimately including the individual will itself. So, while rational apologetics of an evidential or presuppositional sort are of course important, we should not confine ourselves to those lines of argument alone in reaching out to people.

For it is *human beings* whom we are trying to reach, not machines or purely rational creatures who are likely simply to audit the evidence before them and on that ground make an existential commitment. Human beings carry around with them a lot of *pain*. There is a galaxy of hurt swirling around inside the psyche of everyone we meet, and it is this suffering, and the grief, anxiety, anger, confusion, hate, and fear it yields, that bind so many non-Christians to the ultimately frustrating outlook on life that they have—often without a deliberate decision—embraced.

In just one summer at a local cafe I frequented, I met three people (all non-Christians, I would later come to find out) who were experiencing intense pain in their lives. All of these people were friendly, intelligent individuals who outwardly appeared like everyone else, but each was experiencing a profound and unique pain that had them locked into patterns of thinking and feeling that were preventing them from understanding God's love for them, and accepting how it could change their lives. William, a high school counselor, was a recovering alcoholic who—years earlier—as a young adult driven to homelessness by alcohol, had been left to die in a snowbank by his own father, who, while walking through their small Northeastern town one winter, had come across his son on the streets, and just walked on by. Monica, an unemployed thirty-five-year-old mother of three young children, was enduring a nasty divorce proceeding, and had just been evicted from her apartment because, she was told, her kids were too loud for the neighbors. Steven, an engineer, was living alone in a trailer park, while his wife, who divorced him two years ago, was threatening to move out of state with their two young daughters, whom he already saw very infrequently. For each of these individuals, the pain and frustration of their lives was front and center in their consciousness; it was all they could see. Any effort to speak to them of the possibility of a peace that surpasses all human understanding (Phil 4:7) would have to start at that existential place.

This all underscores again the imperative of showing through our character and conduct that it matters to us how they fare in their daily lives. We have to care about them. Emotion, though rightly discounted as a governing principle of knowledge or ethics, is nonetheless the currency of our time. Those who wish to do "existential business" must learn to responsibly and sensitively trade with it.

Seventh, the Christian engaged in personal evangelism in these politically acrimonious and ideologically charged times must emphasize that the decision to come to faith in Christ is utterly apolitical and is essentially a *personal* one that an individual reaches, first, *because it's true*, but then for the best interests of him or herself. To embrace the Lord of life is a decision and then a journey that one makes for *oneself*, and not to join a political party or movement, or to become a part of some other cause or organization. The kingdom of God radically transcends human institutions, ideologies, politics, and personalities. God and the truths of the gospel surpass human history, events, and time itself.

To emphasize this idea is not only wise but also practical, as there are no doubt many people in these polarized times who shrink at the prospect of Christian commitment because they feel that they would then become "one of those," whatever "those" may be in their minds: a member of the "religious right,"

Part I: Theological Topics

a "fundamentalist," a "Jesus Freak," a "right-wing extremist," a Republican. The question "What will the neighbors think?" weighs heavily on people's minds in matters religious, too, and it is the task of the believer to emphasize the utter singularity and apolitical nature of Christian commitment, and the distinction between humble, genuine faith in Christ and the various public examples of that faith, which are sometimes quite unappealing.

Of course, as we have said, Christianity is an all-encompassing faith that pervades all of one's life and being. Thus, there are of course myriad inferences about values, psychology, ethics, and politics to be drawn from Bible-based Christian commitment, and certainly not all of those inferences on any given subject will be of equal cogency. Still though, faith comes first, and then reflection on the other topics follows.

Eighth, I think it's helpful to periodically remind yourself you are a stranger in this world. Yes, this world is not your true and final home, and even though you are in this world, you are not of it (John 17:14, 16). You ought not be shaped and conditioned by this world in such a way that it mainly constitutes your identity. You can't help your social and cultural placement, but remember your values and ultimate commitments are not derived from society and culture; they are derived preeminently from Scripture, and secondarily from the reflections and ideas of Christian thinkers and writers of the past. Tradition is a valuable source for important insights, always tested against the straight edge of God's word. Don't let yourself become so acculturated, so tuned in to popular culture in all its aspects, that you are submerged in its details, in its ethos. You should never really feel at home here; there should always be a sense within you that you were ultimately made for a new and different place, a kingdom not of this earth. For indeed, you were.

Ninth, Tim, in your apologetics, remember that your message is a Jesus-centered message. The incarnate, crucified, resurrected Son of God is the central focus of the Christian faith. And, of course, there is no redemption without him (Acts 4:12). To bear Christian witness means to tell what you have seen of Jesus with the eyes of your faith—as well as the tools of your mind. You are not leading people to join an organization, or to find merely psychological or emotional comfort. You are not showing people a helpful "life hack." You are seeking to introduce them to the Jesus of history, who lived, died, and rose again, and will someday return to rule on earth. Jesus Christ, the preincarnate Logos, the eternal Son of God, that is who you know as your Savior, and it is his divine love and mercy that you are sharing with others. He is the Lord of life, and in him and him alone will peace and personal human fulfillment be found.

Lastly, Tim, I think we have to carefully search our hearts and minds whenever we contemplate or commence engaging in individual evangelism. Are we sharing the Christian message out of an authentic concern for the wellbeing of the other person, or are we driven by our own pride or some other selfish desire? Do we want them to agree with us about Christ because it will make us feel better about ourselves, or make us feel superior to them? Do we want them to agree with us because it will feel like an argumentative victory or personal conquest for us? Unfortunately, our own motives for the things we do, even witnessing, are sometimes complex and hidden from us. We would do well to search our own souls then, and ensure that we are not polluted by motivations that are contrary to the very spirit of the gospel and God.

Remember, Tim, as I said, people need to sense you genuinely care about them before your words, however cogent, will mean much to them. People don't care what you know until they know that you care. Always pray that God will open the hearts and minds of others, but also pray that God will soften your own heart and give you a real concern and empathy for the people you are speaking to. We should pray that we will become the kind of people who truly care about others, and are ready to stand with them once they begin their own journey of faith in the God who made them and loves them with an everlasting love.

Part I: Theological Topics

SONG TO SAVOR:

"When I Survey the Wondrous Cross" by Isaac Watts, arranged by Nathan Drake.[4]

PRAYER:

O Lord, help me to show your love to others with the way I live, and the words I speak. Help me to truly care about them, and to convey to them with simplicity and clarity your saving work in Christ. May those I speak with sense the truth of the message I bring, and give them a sense of urgency about believing it. Bring them to yourself, O God, through the work you have done and are doing within their lives, amen.

MEMORIZE:

> Therefore, if anyone is in Christ, the new creation has come: The old has gone, the new is here! All this is from God, who reconciled us to himself through Christ and gave us the ministry of reconciliation: that God was reconciling the world to himself in Christ, not counting people's sins against them. And he has committed to us the message of reconciliation. We are therefore Christ's ambassadors, as though God were making his appeal through us. We implore you on Christ's behalf: Be reconciled to God. God made him who had no sin to be sin for us, so that in him we might become the righteousness of God. (2 Cor 5:17–21)

SUGGESTED READING:

Chan, Sam. *Evangelism in a Skeptical World: How to Make the Unbelievable News About Jesus More Believable*. Grand Rapids: Zondervan, 2018.

Moon, Jay W., and W. Bud Simon. *Effective Intercultural Evangelism: Good News in a Diverse World*. Downers Grove, IL: InterVarsity, 2021.

---

4. Watts, "When I Survey."

Newbigin, Leslie. *The Gospel in a Pluralist Society*. Grand Rapids: Eerdmans, 1989.

Packer, J. I. *Evangelism and the Sovereignty of God*. Downers Grove, IL: InterVarsity, 2012.

Scroggins, Jimmy, et al. *Turning Everyday Conversations into Gospel Conversations*. Nashville: B & H, 2016.

5

Grief

"Losing a loved one is like having your house burn down; it takes years to realize all that you've lost."
—Mark Twain

"No one ever told me that grief felt so like fear. I am not afraid, but the sensation is like being afraid. The same fluttering in the stomach, the same restlessness, the yawning. I keep on swallowing."
—C. S. Lewis

"I sat with my anger long enough until she told me her real name was grief."
—C. S. Lewis

From: thebradstetson@gmail.com
To: Gretchen

Gretchen, thank you for your note. I'm sorry about your dear grandmother's passing. She sounds like a great lady, and she was blessed with a wonderful, long life. But I know that doesn't make it any easier to lose her. "The longer you have them the more you miss them," I've heard it said. Often, it seems, college-aged students experience the death of a grandparent, and quite possibly it is their first experience with the death of a family member.

I have known Christians who seem to feel obligated not to feel deeply sad or bereaved about the death of a family member. They seem to think that because they're confident their loved one went to heaven, and that their loved one is living everlasting life in joy there, that it is improper or faithless for them to be sad.

I strongly disagree with that attitude. It's OK for Christians to grieve, and to grieve deeply. The psychological, emotional, spiritual, and even physical dimensions of grief affect every human being, irrespective of religious commitments. Of course it's important to remember we do not grieve without hope, and that heaven is real, and that by God's grace in Christ you will see your grandma again, and be with her. But all of that doesn't change the reality that you miss her a lot right now, and are in a lot of pain at her passing. That's normal. So go ahead and grieve, and let the tears flow. That's not to say that you should nurture and cultivate your grief, and hang on to it every day. Some people make that mistake. But let it take its natural course, and let yourself feel the pain of loss. In time you will integrate the pain of her passing into the rest of your life, so that it is a painful part of a healthy and happy whole, which is what she would want for you.[1]

I want to suggest to you ten practical actions you can take to help yourself move through grief and embrace the life you have as one that has loved and lost. As you consider these practices, Gretchen, keep top of mind your overarching Christian worldview, and God's tender, abiding love for you amidst every circumstance you experience.

The old saying is true: "If there is an elephant in the room, introduce him." No good purpose is served by denial, yet we are very good at it. And when it comes to facing the pain of our grief with eyes open, we often turn away instead. Painful thought it is, it's important to acknowledge that we are hurting because of loss.

---

1. The single best book about grief from a Christian perspective that I know of is Sittser, *Grace Disguised*.

Part I: Theological Topics

I think this is a helpful first step. This acknowledgment does not show a lack of faith; on the contrary, it shows humility. When we have a psychological elephant in the room of our mind, we should acknowledge him and plan a way to shrink him down to a manageable size, then get him on his way. I think we should be honest about the pain of our grief, and resolve going forward to be proactive, and do the necessary grief work to begin addressing the elephant in the room. That is a small but significant beginning.

Second, write yourself a comforting and encouraging letter. Imagine you had a friend for whom you cared deeply, and imagine that friend just experienced the death of someone they love very much. You would want to help them, comfort them, and encourage them. Now substitute yourself for that friend. You are worthy of being comforted and encouraged, too. Write yourself a letter saying the same things you would say to a good friend. Then, read the letter, put it away for a few days, then read it again. Do this for a few weeks and then write yourself a second letter, and so on. This is an act of self-compassion, treating yourself as gently as you would treat someone else. Avoid thinking you are so "strong" or "solid" that you don't need help and tender compassion. That is a misunderstanding of strength and personal fortitude. Feeling intense sorrow and bereavement is not a sign of weakness; to the contrary, it is a sign of deep humanity and personal capacity to love.

Third, buy a big calendar, and use it. One problem bereaved people face is the feeling that one day drags into the next, always the same. Grieving people also sometimes are pressured by well-meaning people into doing activities they really don't want to do. An "appointment calendar" can solve both of those problems. Large calendars, like a desk calendar, give you room to write. So sit down with the calendar and start filling your days with appointments. Appointments with whom? Most importantly, with yourself. Without taking yourself out of social circulation, you can pen in valuable "self-time." The simple act of reserving time for yourself empowers you to breathe and reflect. Appointments like "movie with me" or "journaling with me" make it possible for you to always tell others, when asked to go somewhere or do something,

"Let me check my calendar, I may have an appointment." This way you can decline in a socially graceful way. If you want to accept someone's invitation, you can always break an appointment with yourself. Using a calendar in this way helps you to gain a feeling of control over your time, and it gives you a feeling of structure at this difficult period in your life.

I have a big desk calendar like that, and I use it all the time. In fact, I carry it with me wherever I go. This was, of course, a source of great embarrassment to my children when they were little. To walk into a Starbucks with your father is bad enough, but if he's carrying a giant desk calendar with all kinds of scribbles on it, it's even worse. I like the calendar because I can see the whole month at a glance, and an iPhone is just too small for me to see, and too hard for my shaky hands to operate. Anyway, I find a desk calendar can be a very useful and comforting companion. And, it gives you the chance to check what's coming tomorrow, or next week, and pray about it in advance.

Fourth, move your body; move your mind. As you adjust to your life without the physical presence of your loved one who died, it's vital you get outside and move. Notice I didn't say "exercise," since for some people that sounds daunting. There is no need to make it a big undertaking. You don't have to join a gym, or buy some new clothes. Pick short, achievable goals, like a short hike, a walk around the block, a bike ride to the park. Keep these jaunts short, as this will give you a sense of accomplishment, and you will derive the physical and psychological benefits of having enlisted your body in your ongoing encounter with grief.

Fifth, realize that you do not need to "understand" your grief right now. When I coached Little League, I established the One Minute Rule. It was this: If anyone gets hit by a baseball, whatever the person hit by the ball says for the first minute after being hit is OK. Screaming and accusations were common after being hit by the baseball, but everyone knew that you got a free pass for a minute. And they knew that after a minute the person had to pull themselves together and be ready to move on. Well, bereaved people get a lot longer than a minute, or a month, or a year, to integrate their experience into the rest of their outlook on life, and to understand it in the context of their Christian faith. So don't feel anxiety about fully grasping what has happened to you. The Holy Spirit will comfort you, time will help clear your mind, and you will eventually be able to address your loss, the pain it has brought you, and the changes in your life that have ensued.

Sixth, decide that in the times to come, you will begin to focus a bit more on others as a part of your loved one's legacy. This is a valuable change you can make in your life. We all need to get out of ourselves and focus on other people and their problems. Sometimes, this helps us gain a fresh perspective on our own life. As you do this, you will no doubt talk with new people, and when the opportunity presents itself, tell them about your loved one who has died. You don't have to tell your loved one's life story or anything like that; just mention them in passing. You may feel more comfortable talking about your loved one with people who didn't know him or her, and it is valuable to begin to talk out loud, in the past tense, about your loved one. It may be shocking to hear yourself talk about them in the past tense, but that will help you integrate their death into your life. You can be sure that others have also felt the pain of losing a loved one. God will bring you to people who can benefit from your story. Who knows, God may well bring something beautiful into your life as you seek to serve others.

Seventh, listen to the music. A recent study I saw asserted that sad people who listen to their favorite music that matches their mood report feeling better.[2] Music is therapeutic and soothing. Throughout history, music has been central to the expression of human values and sentiments. Make a short list of some songs—of any kind—that you have always liked. Then go to YouTube.com and listen to them or order them online. You can create your own playlist, too. Just get the music playing so you can listen. As you do, let your mind take you where it will, and after a while I'll bet you'll feel relaxed and maybe even renewed.

Eighth, know that your loved one is wishing you well. Even though they are in heaven now, they still remember you. In a quiet

---

2. Latorre, "How Music Affects Your Mood."

moment, write down a few notes about what you think your loved one would want for you now. Trouble imagining what that might be? It's probably the same you would wish for your loved one, had you been the one that died. Make a list of a few states of mind, attitudes, or commodities that your loved one would want for you to attain as you move forward without them. For example, my husband would want me to look toward the future and not be paralyzed by mourning. Or, my sister would want me to buy those expensive boots we used to talk about, or my grandmother would want me to go on a cruise. Then, choose one of those outcomes and pursue it. Look back at your list after a few months, and check off the outlook or object you now have. Deliberately choose to achieve something you think your loved one would want you to have. By doing so, you will honor their memory.

Ninth, always remember the good times. No doubt you have a treasure trove of positive, happy memories of the person you have loved and lost. By making a list of your positive memories—the cruise, the fiftieth-anniversary dinner, the annual trips to your favorite getaway spot, the long drives you used to take—you remind yourself of all that you gained by having that person in your life. And those gains, those happy experiences you had, you will never lose. They are locked in to your human experience and consciousness. They are a part of you. If you can create a list of happy memories and experiences, you will gain a sense of gratitude for how wonderful your life has been. And that attitude of gratitude will be a powerfully positive force in your life. Gratitude will help soothe the pain of your grief, and remind you of how wonderful life can be, and of how wonderful your life is.

Tenth, take it to the Lord in prayer. Make a habit of going to God and telling him that your heart is hurting. Talk to him like you would talk to a close friend, and tell him about your grief. Pour out your heart to him, and tell him you need his help, which you do. (The Psalms, like Pss 64 and 34, are full of those kind of examples.) Of course you always need his help, but it's still a good idea to explicitly tell him this, especially when you are in the stress of grief. Ask him to help you and strengthen you. Ask him to encourage

Part I: Theological Topics

you and empower you, and enable you to grow through your grief so that you become someone who can help other people who are enduring the pain of bereavement. Implore him to enlarge your heart, so that it can embrace the sufferings of other people. That is a prayer God will answer, so keep watch to notice what he does.

So often we think of grief as something that happens to us instead of something we do. This is unfortunate, since passivity and inaction will not help us to engage the new reality of loss in our lives. This is not to say that grief is a "problem" we can solve, or a "condition" we can make go away, but it is to say that we can be active participants in our emotional wellbeing. By purposefully facing our sorrow, and calmly, carefully thinking about what we can do to help integrate our sorrow into our larger life, we can contribute to forging our new identity. And this is a powerful choice to make as our new lives come to us. And surely the Great Comforter, the Holy Spirit, will be with us every step of the way.[3]

From: thebradstetson@gmail.com
To: Gretchen

Thank you, Gretchen, for asking me to comment on a personal experience of loss I have had. I appreciate your interest in seeking an example of how to talk about grief in the first person. I think the best way to go about it is to simply go about it, that is, just tell your own story. My story of the stillbirth of our first child is at once unique, yet common. Stillbirth is a strange kind of loss that most people don't have to endure. And yet, it happens a lot more than you might think. The last time I checked, in the US about one in 175 babies are stillborn.[4]

The choking grief brought on by the death of one's child has always been one of the strongest challenges to religious faith. This is particularly the case with a calamity like stillbirth. It is a uniquely disorienting tragedy, ambushing parents with a cruel paradox: death before life, the ending before the beginning, a funeral instead

---

3. On this general idea, see Elliot, *Suffering Is Never for Nothing*.
4. March of Dimes, "Stillbirth."

of a christening, the stale pall of death over the young body of new life, a first hello as a final goodbye.

After our son B. J. was stillborn in 1991, my wife and I—like so many other parents who have lost children at birth or early in life—were sentenced to a lifetime of mystery. Who would he have become? What would he have done with his life? We were condemned not only to grief, but to curiosity. To this day, my wife will cry every time she hears the Christmas song "Greensleeves," also called "What Child Is This?"And in never knowing him and how he might have lived, we also lost a measure of self-knowledge and intimacy with one another. We would never find out who we each might have become as his father and mother, how his life would have caused us to change and grow.

In child loss, the observation of grief often attributed to Mark Twain is most true: "Losing a loved one is like having your house burn down; it takes years to realize all that you've lost." Indeed, through the years the tendrils of grief can creep into the soul, altering one's psyche and relationships in mysterious ways.

For example, the American presidency has become a sort of public illustration of this phenomenon. Abraham Lincoln and Calvin Coolidge each bore the immense stress of losing young sons while in office. John F. Kennedy and Ronald Reagan both had their already complex characters enduringly altered by neonatal death. George H. W. Bush could never discuss the death of his three-year-old daughter without a tearful, inarticulate stammering. Joe Biden's loss of his wife and daughter in a car accident became the central biographical fact of his life, and an important part of his political identity and character.

From the melancholia of Lincoln and the rueful taciturnity of Coolidge to the reckless hedonism of Kennedy, the strange familial detachment of Reagan, the inexpressible pain of George H. W. Bush, and the emotional transparency of Joe Biden, we see in these men's demeanors the reverberations of soul trauma. The mourning of parents who have lost children reminds us that the terrain of the psyche is not as well charted as we like to believe. The twenty-first century sees us mapping the brain and reading DNA, yet the dark and tortuous tunnels of trauma into which great loss conducts us remain largely unexplored, and not well understood.

What, then, is the human soul to do? Can the oppressive weight of such loss be lifted? For the believing heart, the answer is a courageous "yes." For amid the desolation of loss, a redemptive paradox emerges: by being reduced, we grow. In the experience of being cut back to the root of our selves, we find a concentrated clarity in the nature of our humanity. We see our finitude, vulnerability, and deeper immateriality. We sense more urgently than we otherwise do the inherent void within us that cannot be filled but by the healing embrace of the One who, being personal yet infinite, is alone able to integrate and bring meaning to our bewildering human experience. The flaming sorrow of grief becomes the Refiner's fire, consuming spiritual dross, leaving behind only understanding that cannot be burned. And in its purity, that substance of soul becomes a new and utterly priceless treasure. Profound loss brings a strange point of contact with the ultimate purposes of life, with the true nature of living and the fantastic reality of the hereafter. Indeed, intense sorrow may well be one of the more under-recognized phenomena supporting the plausibility of God's existence. It is itself a "signal of transcendence," a clue to us that the material world is a weak explanation for human experience, and that the supernatural world beyond death is as real—or more so—than anything we know. That certainly is the biblical point of view.[5]

For most people, the initial response to child loss is a rage against God for allowing such tragedy to befall them. I certainly felt that way. Yet why should this be, unless we have a reason to believe matters ought to be different? It is more than the unusualness or untimeliness of child loss that so provokes us to shake our mortal fists at the Most High. We are moved by the violation of the inner analogy to the transcendent that the parent-child relationship represents. As we are designed to mature toward the Divine, so our children are intended to be intimately with us for years. We

---

5. See Berger, *Rumor of Angels*. For an excellent and more contemporary discussion of the rediscovery of the supernatural, see Dreher, *Living in Wonder*.

perceive our relationship to our children is more than physiological and emotional. It is a bonding of soul.

Thus, the jolt we experience at their death speaks to us of the metaphysical by heightening our awareness of it. The turmoil of intense sorrow can propel us up to the limits of this world, providing us a hint of the larger order, an ecstatic suspicion that there is an ultimate purpose beyond the dimness of our today.

The truth lying beneath my own grief, Gretchen, is that I never felt closer to God than I did in the months after my son died. The end of his life eventually led me to discover a fresh fullness in my own life, and a new knowledge that it is but a preamble to the greatest discovery that awaits us all.

About eight years after my son B. J.'s stillbirth I wrote about the experience in my book *Tender Fingerprints: A True Story of Loss and Resolution*.[6] For years after its publication, I would get letters occasionally from women who had had a similar experience. They would tell their story, which is inherently therapeutic I think, and then they would thank me for telling my story, and say it helped them in some way. It was of course deeply gratifying to hear that, and to know that my own loss had been helpful in some way to someone else. God used my loss and my story to have a redemptive impact in someone else's life.

It was always thrilling to realize that, Gretchen, and I want you to know he is doing the same in your life. Yes, the pains and griefs and disappointments—of all kinds—that you will experience will become compassionate tools in the Master's hands, instruments that he uses to heal the wounds of other hurting people you talk with. Your story, and your testimony of faith in the face of suffering, will inspire others, and remind them that God walks with them through every fiery trial of their lives. That knowledge is precious indeed, and life-giving to the soul.

---

6. Stetson, *Tender Fingerprints*.

PART I: THEOLOGICAL TOPICS

SONG TO SAVOR:

"Scars in Heaven" by Mark Hall and Matthew West, sung by Casting Crowns.[7]

PRAYER:

O God, I come to you broken and in pain. Please hold me in your merciful and loving arms, and heal my hurting heart. Help me to walk with you in this valley, and help me to learn to trust in you and turn to you every hour of every day. I know you understand the pain and sorrow of my grief, and I ask you to strengthen me and encourage me by your Holy Spirit. Be with me now and always, amen.

MEMORIZE:

> Where O Death is your victory? Where O Death is your sting? . . . Thanks be to God! He gives us the victory through our Lord Jesus Christ.
> —1 Cor 15:55–57

SUGGESTED READING:

Guthrie, Nancy. *Holding On to Hope: A Pathway Through Suffering to the Heart of God*. Carol Stream, IL: Tyndale, 2002.
Keller, Timothy. *Walking with God Through Pain and Suffering*. New York: Penguin, 2015.
O'Malley, Patrick, and Tim Madigan. *Getting Grief Right: Finding Your Story of Love in the Sorrow of Loss*. Louisville, CO: Sounds True, 2017.
Sittser, Gerald. *A Grace Disguised: How the Soul Grows Through Loss*. Grand Rapids: Zondervan, 1996.
Vroegop, Mark. *Dark Clouds, Deep Mercy: Discovering the Grace of Lament*. Wheaton, IL: Crossway, 2019.

---

7. Casting Crowns, "Scars in Heaven."

6

Music

"Next to the Word of God, the noble art of music is the greatest treasure in the world."

—Martin Luther

"Music is a higher revelation than all wisdom and philosophy."

—Ludwig van Beethoven

"The books or the music in which we thought the beauty was located will betray us if we trust to them; it was not in them, it only came through them, and what came through them was longing. . . . .For they are not the thing in itself; they are only the scent of a flower we have not found, the echo of a tune we have not heard, news from a country we have never yet visited."

—C. S. Lewis

From: thebradstetson@gmail.com
To: Sandi

Yes, I remember you singing "In Christ Alone" at the chapel service before I spoke, you were great! It's a great contemporary hymn,

Part I: Theological Topics

with excellent theology. Sometimes I just read the words over; they are a great Bible lesson in themselves. There are a lot of songs like that out there. You asked what I thought about the role of music as a tool in the Christian life, and I think you point to an important and significant topic.

First, to music itself. It is of course one of the most universal and powerful of human expressions. From ancient chants to contemporary music in all its manifestations, music is a big part of a lot of people's lives. It's also been a big part of human religious expression. As the historian of religion Robert S. Ellwood wrote:

> Music is virtually universal as an important accompaniment of religion, except in Islam in which chanting and rhythmic recitation take its place. Music's importance in facilitating the basic task of religious symbolism helping the participant to make the transition from ordinary to sacred reality, is unsurpassed. . . . [Music] in religious worship sets the altered emotional tone and universe of meaning of the rite and does much to bring the participant into it.[1]

And certainly throughout Christian history, music has been central to the expression of our faith. From the Psalms to the hymns of the early church to medieval chants to the music of the Reformation, the Great Awakening, the experience of black slaves in North America, and all the way up to today, song has been the voice of faith, its expression, and inspiration. We were made to praise God, literally, and so the satisfaction and calm and joy we feel when we sing out to him makes complete sense. I have a Basset Hound, and he loves to go on walks and track scents. When he catches an interesting scent on a walk, he's off to the races, and he bays with delight. He's doing what he was made to do, and so it is with us when we worship God. We are fulfilling our most basic and most ultimate purpose.

But beyond that, I can suggest to you five reasons I think music is such an essential tool for the Christian walk. Most obviously, music is important for us because it can do so much. Music

---

1. Ellwood, *Introducing Religion*, 110.

can motivate, heal, and comfort. So often athletes and others in training turn to music for motivation to complete their workout, and it can inspire us too as we seek to grow in our faith. Music can also heal and comfort. So many studies have shown the healing, relaxing, and comforting power of music.[2] There's even an academic journal devoted to the subject called the *Journal of Music Therapy*. Listening to our favorite praise songs or hymns, or any special song, can so often bring a feeling of relaxation and peace.[3] So much so, I'd say a favorite song and a few deep breaths can do as much to lower blood pressure and calm our minds than any medicine can. It seems when you listen to contemporary music on the radio, and also so many other types of music, you realize that when something is important to people, they put it to music. Love, loss, disappointment, joy, these all are themes of not only pop songs, but also Broadway songs, opera, and songs of faith as well. Music is the universal language for human beings, the *lingua franca* of the soul that always serves to convey and console our deepest sentiments.

Second, music can aid us in prayer because it can help put us in a prayerful mood. To listen to one of your favorite praise songs before starting to pray can help not only focus your mind, but it can help calm you down. It can slow the pace of your thoughts to bring you into a more reflective, meditative mindset. With so many distractions everywhere in our world every minute of the day, this preparatory role music can play before we bring our praise and petitions to God is very valuable.

Third, the right kind of music can have a cleansing effect on our souls. It can remind us again of our priorities and bring clarity to our minds, which are so overcome by the shadows and storms of our hectic days. The Psalms, which were written as songs, can serve this purpose so well. Singing your favorite psalm to whatever tune you make up yourself is a great way to focus on the words of that psalm, and be transported to a place of repentance and

---

2. See Zaatar et al., "Transformative Power of Music."

3. Remember how David played the harp for Saul when Saul was distressed by an evil spirit, and Saul felt relief and peace. See 1 Sam 16:14–23.

reconsideration. The late Christian singer Keith Green once wrote a beautiful version of Ps 51 that can be found at YouTube.com. It's called "Create in Me a Clean Heart," and listening to it is a wonderful way to absorb the meaning of that psalm.

Fourth, singing at church or in a group setting can provide a strong sense of community. A group of believers singing the words of their faith together can be a very powerful expression of solidarity. We can experience the reality that we are not alone, and that the Christian life is not lived in isolation, nor is it meant to be. I remember I once went to a "Promise Keepers" event at the Los Angeles Memorial Coliseum back in the 1990s. "Promise Keepers" was an organization dedicated to helping men be responsible and godly husbands and fathers. During a time of worship, on the coliseum's jumbotron were the lyrics to Martin Luther's hymn "A Mighty Fortress." All 70,000 or so men in the coliseum stood and sang out a contemporary version of that song together, singing Luther's lyrics. I looked around the stadium and felt how inspiring it was to be with tens of thousands of other like-minded men. So, song can really connect us with one another, as it amounts to common confession of our shared aspirations and purpose.

Lastly, Sandi, I think the songs of faith we have loved can serve as signposts or markers to us of where we have been in our Christian walk. Ten years ago there may have been a song that really spoke to you and conveyed your aspirations and intent as a young Christian. But through the years new music came along, and you sort of lost touch with that old song, the way you might with an old friend. But then either on YouTube or some other way you encounter that song again, and like an old picture in an album, it takes you back to what you were like at that time, and what your faith was like. I was browsing some old songs on YouTube the other day, and an algorithm brought up an old song by the Christian singer Amy Grant called "I Have Decided to Follow Jesus." It reminded me of my life as a young Christian then, and of the desire I had to follow Jesus first.

So, Sandi, music can do so much for us; we really need to integrate it into our lives as Christians, and make it a partner with us as we walk with God.[4] So much music in the world today seems either harsh or vapid; there's just nothing like a great tune with clear lyrics that conveys solid, inspiring theology. A simple song like that can accomplish a lot.

SONG TO SAVOR:

"Heart of Worship" by Matt Redman.[5]

PRAYER:

O God, bring to my awareness songs of praise that will speak to my heart of your goodness and greatness. Bring music to me that will help me grow in you and toward you, and that will inspire me to remember your love and mercy, and your everlasting kindness. Amen.

MEMORIZE:

> Praise God in his sanctuary; praise him in his mighty heavens. Praise him for his acts of power; praise him for his surpassing greatness. Praise him with the sounding of the trumpet, praise him with the harp and lyre, praise him with timbrel and dancing, praise him with the strings and pipe, praise him with the clash of cymbals, praise him with resounding cymbals. Let everything that has breath praise the Lord. (Ps 150:1–6)

SUGGESTED READING:

Aniol, Scott. *Worship in Song: A Biblical Philosophy of Music and Worship*. Winona Lake, IN: BMH, 2009.

---

4. For a classic statement on music and the Christian life, see Elmore, "Place of Music."

5. Redman, "Heart of Worship."

Part I: Theological Topics

Brown, Michael L. *The Power of Music: God's Call to Change the World One Song at a Time*. Lake Mary, FL: Charisma, 2019.

Lefebvre, Michael. *Singing the Songs of Jesus: Revisiting the Psalms*. Fearn: Christian Focus, 2011.

Levitin, Daniel. *I Heard There Was a Secret Chord: Music as Medicine*. New York: Norton, 2024.

Lynch, Danielle Anne. *God in Sound and Silence: Music as Theology*. Eugene, OR: Pickwick, 2018.

7
The Demonic

"Satan would love nothing more than for you and I to pretend he doesn't exist or acknowledge his existence and take his assault on you lightly. He would also like to see you buckle under fear at his threats or defend yourself using worldly and man-made tactics."

—Randy Smith

"There are two equal and opposite errors into which our race can fall about the devils. One is to disbelieve in their existence. The other is to believe, and to feel an excessive and unhealthy interest in them. They themselves are equally pleased by both errors and hail a materialist or a magician with the same delight."

—C. S. Lewis

"Through pride the devil became the devil. Pride leads to every vice, it's the complete anti-God state of mind."

—C. S. Lewis

Part I: Theological Topics

From: thebradstetson@gmail.com
To: Martin

Thank you for your question, Martin, and most definitely, no, I don't think you are silly to believe that demons are real, and that they are active in our world. They are indeed.

I remember when I lectured at universities, sometimes the question of suicide would come up. I was always very reluctant to say almost anything about it, and in fact I said very little. I always quickly changed the subject. And that was because, in the first place, I was not an expert, and in the second place, it was the nature of the topic that dwelling upon it and talking about it could invariably lead someone toward it. And with such a dangerous and deadly act, I didn't want to be responsible for even suggesting to someone that they give it a second or third thought.

Well, that's how I feel about this topic, too. It's an important topic, and I commend you for wanting to understand something about this topic, but it is a subject that wisdom dictates we only touch upon, and leave the detailed investigations to others with far more experience and insight. Every Christian must be, as Peter says, "alert and of sober mind," on guard against our demonic adversary (1 Pet 5:8). But we also must remember that our calling and life is in walking with Jesus, and as we do so we will naturally crowd out the deceptions of the devil, and defeat him without giving him a thought. Our attentions should be directed upward, not downward.

Regarding the demonic, Martin, first let me say that I do believe we in the West are emerging out of our materialist fog and into a fuller recognition of the nonmaterial and the nonnatural, in other words, the supernatural. And certainly if you were to look at arts and entertainment since World War II, including the television and internet worlds, you will find an ever more intense interest in the supernatural. Given human nature, this interest is usually in the dark and demonic, but there have been plenty of good and God-ward looking offerings too. It's too bad that moving through the third decade of the twenty-first century, so much

The Demonic

of our cultural interest in the supernatural is in the demonic. For remember, Jesus is a lot more interesting than Satan.

But, Martin, I want to lay down some ideas for you, some polestars that can guide your Christian life as you live it, and as you come upon the demonic.

First, let's just frankly acknowledge demons are real. Demons are fallen angels that truly exist. To say that "demons are real" would have got you laughed out of serious company for a good part of the nineteenth and twentieth centuries, and still even today. It is a capital irony that in the age of space exploration, the digital revolution, and hyper-technology, there is a return to interest in what has been regarded as the primitivism of the demonic. But we have become victims of our much learning. We have been educated into ignorance of the fullness of reality. It was the German biblical scholar of the early and mid-twentieth century, Rudolf Bultmann, who epitomized the intellectual class's contempt for the supernatural when he said, "We cannot use electric light and radios . . . and at the same time believe in the spirit and wonder world of the New Testament."[1] This, while his truculent homeland was in thrall to genocide and world war, episodes of history that were quintessentially demonic.

But the demonic and the angelic and God's sometimes miraculous work in the world are all real, and it seems to me the ubiquity of resurgent interest in them is a testimony of sorts to that fact.[2]

But second, Martin, I must stress and hasten to add that we ought not seek them out, nor even—most of us—study intently the topic of the demonic. As I said, Jesus is a lot more interesting, and a lot more important, than Satan. There are some doors we just should not open, some places we just should not go. It isn't only cats that idle curiosity has killed. Scripture has within it all we really need to know about the demonic, and in fact it is the Bible which is the only truly reliable source of information on the topic. So don't fall prey to the overweening interest of contemporary culture, with its nightly and relentless "paranormal" investigations

1. Bultmann, *New Testament and Mythology*, 4.
2. This resurgence is discussed at length in Dreher, *Living in Wonder*.

Part I: Theological Topics

and cinematic glorifications of spirits, demons, and devils. In fact, Martin, as a practice, if you are watching TV and a commercial for such a program comes on, change the channel; don't even watch the commercial. And if you are watching some show and an indulgence in witchcraft or other spiritually dark enterprise begins to be displayed, change the channel. This is a great habit to develop. There are some topics it's good to be somewhat ignorant about, and this is one of them. If you read C. S. Lewis' *The Screwtape Letters* plus your Bible, you'll know more than enough about the demonic to successfully honor God in your life.

Third, let me say there is actually a very important spiritual principle that underlays this great sense of caution we must exercise around this topic. It is simply this: Persons go where they are wanted. If you think about it, you see that this principle governs much of our lives. We talk with people who want to talk with us, we form friendships with people who want to be friends with us, and we go places to which we are invited. We are comfortable where we are wanted, and we are not comfortable where we are not wanted.

So it is spiritually. Spiritual personalities—demons, angels, God—respond to invitations for association. God wants us to call upon him, and he wants us to draw near to him. And in turn he hears us, and draws near to us. As we reach out to God through prayer or reading his word, he communes with us through his Holy Spirit.

Demons, too, go where they are wanted. If a door is opened for them, they may well enter. The Ouija board is perhaps the best known invitation to the demonic, but there are others too, such as psychedelic drugs and immersive studies in the occult. And increasingly, thoughtful writers like Rod Dreher are sounding the alarm that the rapidly advancing super-technology of AI (artificial intelligence) can be a vector for the demonic. It is a stunning and unexpected point of view, but one with growing currency among Christian intellectuals. (UFOs and alien manifestations, too, are quickly coming to be regarded as demonic realties.)[3] Even *The*

---

3. See Rod Dreher's Substack newletter for his regular discussions of artificial intelligence as a demonic tool. For representative discussion see Dreher's

Atlantic Monthly, the flagship publication of American mainstream materialism and leftism, ran an article about the demonic potentials of artificial intelligence.[4] I mention this to you, Martin, not to alarm you (or to elicit giggles from you), but to alert you to these emerging concerns. Remember, the wisdom of this world will be confounded by God's ways, and the plausibility structures and the official story of our world are sure to be blind to the spiritual truths that shatter their validity. There is no reason to believe that the mysterious and unexplained phenomena of our time can be grasped and described by the categories of contemporary man.

Fourth, Martin, I do think it's necessary to list at least a few of the personality traits of the demonic, or demons themselves. As it turns out, they really aren't that complicated.

First of all, remember, they are fallen angels, and as such, they are vastly, vastly, more intelligent than we are. I should think human beings are agonizingly boring to demons. So we must never presume to rebuke or confront them on our own power. They have the intelligence of angels, as they are fallen angels. Hence, they can know a lot about us and our lives, and infer a lot as well. They are not omniscient, they don't know the future, and they cannot be an integral part of our lives without some manner of invitation. But their intelligence and cunning are but two traits that make us no match for them. And we must add, they are also very patient compared to us. That is, they've been around since the fall; they know and understand human beings very well. They have seen a lot of us come and go. And so they know how to, over time, wear us down, and even gradually destroy our lives in myriad ways. This is one reason among so many others why it is crucial that we

---

Substack of July 25, 2025, available by subscription only.

Regarding UFOs and unidentified aerial phenomena as demonic manifestations, see the work of Christian astrophysicist Hugh Ross at his apologetics website www.reasons.org. See also the important work of religious studies scholar Diana Pasulka. Her books *American Cosmic* and *Encounters* are essential reading for understanding the supernatural character of UFO and alien sightings and culture.

4. See Shroff, "ChatGPT Gave Instructions."

Part I: Theological Topics

daily, steadily, walk with God, and talk to him in prayer constantly throughout each and every day.

Demons are also selfish and legalistic. They are concerned with themselves and their interests only, and have absolute contempt for us. Their hatred for us cannot be overstated. When it comes to acting in our lives, they will seize upon any opportunity, and claim it as a right to do what they will in our lives. Exorcists report this demonic legalism regularly.[5] We must be vigilant regarding our lifestyles and interests so as not to open doors to them unknowingly, as so many young people have done through carelessly playing with the Ouija board or pursuing other paranormal topics.

And Martin, this cannot be overstated: Demons are liars. This is the most basic and defining characteristic of the demonic. They will lie in every way possible, and in a manner so subtle we cannot detect it. We don't have to understand how they can lie to us to know that they will. Jesus called Satan "the father of lies," and indeed he is (John 8:44). This ability and inclination to mislead and prevaricate is at the very heart of demonic identity, and it is essential to their being. "Liar" is who they are. In fact, as journalist Randall Sullivan has importantly pointed out, the devil's greatest deception is employing all the evil powers of his malevolent existence to convince human beings that he in fact does not really exist. It is the ultimate ontological lie.[6]

Lastly, Martin, I would like to answer the question you posed of "Why?" Why does the devil hate human beings so much? Simply put, it is because we bear the image of the most High God, the God Satan rebelled against, and aspired to overthrow. It must be so outrageous and so annoying to Satan and his demons—to extents we cannot grasp—that human beings are the objects of God's infinite love and action. Think of it: We human beings who are so stupid, so vulgar, so predictable and simple—we yet are the subjects of redemption. God loves *us*, of all creatures. We are the reason God the Son took on human flesh eternally; we are the

---

5. See Martins, *Exorcist Files*.
6. See Sullivan's riveting book, *The Devil's Best Trick*, for exposition.

reason God the Son suffered and died on the cross, and then rose from the dead. We people, who are to demons ridiculously worthless—worthy only of viscous hatred and unrestrained condemnation—are those whom God has favored by loving us so much he gave his Son for us. This really ticks off the devil and his demons. Inside of us is the image of the Holy Trinity, and this makes us a very fitting target for Satan. Indeed, as Luther wrote in his great hymn of 1527, "A Mighty Fortress," we are easy targets apart from God's protection. The opening words of that powerful song are well worth remembering:

> For still our ancient foe Doth seek to work us woe; His craft and pow'r are great And armed with cruel hate; On earth is not his equal; Did we in our own strength confide Our striving would be losing; Were not the right Man on our side The Man of God's own choosing; Dost ask who that may be Christ Jesus it is He; Lord Saboath His name From age to age the same And He must win the battle; And tho' this world with devils filled Should threaten to undo us; We will not fear for God hath willed His truth to triumph thru us; The prince of darkness grim We tremble not for him; His rage we can endure For lo his doom is sure; One little word shall fell him.[7]

So, Martin, be aware of the demonic, but not overly conscious. Resist the attractions of darkness. Your job is to imitate Christ in your life, to walk in the footsteps of Jesus of Nazareth, the God-man. Do that, and the devil will be but an angry spectator.

SONG TO SAVOR:

"A Mighty Fortress" by Martin Luther, arranged by Michael W. Smith.[8]

---

7. Luther, "Might Fortress."
8. Smith, "Mighty Fortress."

Part I: Theological Topics

PRAYER:

O God, protect me from all demonic harm and oppression. Be my shield and shelter, deliver me from evil, and guard me by your heavenly angels. I trust and rest in your strength, Lord, not my own, knowing that greater is he that is in me than he that is in the world. Amen.

MEMORIZE:

> Be alert and of sober mind. Your enemy the devil prowls around like a roaring lion looking for someone to devour. Resist him, standing firm in the faith, because you know that the family of believers throughout the world is undergoing the same kind of sufferings. And the God of all grace, who called you to his eternal glory in Christ, after you have suffered a little while, will himself restore you and make you strong, firm and steadfast. To him be the power for ever and ever. Amen. (1 Pet 5:8–11)

SUGGESTED READING:

Arnold, Clinton. *Powers of Darkness: Principalities and Powers in Paul's Letters*. Downers Grove, IL: InterVarsity, 1992.
Heiser, Michael S. *Demons: What the Bible Really Says About the Powers of Darkness*. Bellingham, WA: Lexham, 2020.
———. *Supernatural: What the Bible Teaches About the Unseen World—and Why It Matters*. Bellingham, WA: Lexham, 2015.
Lewis, C. S. *The Screwtape Letters*. New York: Macmillan, 1961.
Martins, Carlos. *The Exorcist Files*. Brentwood, TN: Faithwords, 2024.

PART II

Social and Ethical Topics

8

Politics

"Of all tyrannies, a tyranny sincerely exercised for the good of its victims may be the most oppressive. It would be better to live under robber barons than under omnipotent moral busybodies. The robber baron's cruelty may sometimes sleep, his cupidity may at some point be satiated; but those who torment us for our own good will torment us without end for they do so with the approval of their own conscience."

—C. S. Lewis

"The modern State exists not to protect our rights but to do us good or make us good—anyway, to do something to us or to make us something. Hence the new name 'leaders' for those who were once 'rulers.' We are less their subjects than their wards, pupils, or domestic animals. There is nothing left of which we can say to them, 'Mind your own business.' Our whole lives are their business."

—C. S. Lewis

"Silence in the face of evil is itself evil: God will not hold us guiltless. Not to speak is to speak. Not to act is to act."

—Dietrich Bonhoeffer

Part II: Social and Ethical Topics

From: thebradstetson@gmail.com
To: Rick and Brian

Thank you, Rick and Brian, for your enthusiastic letter. I think it's great that you're so interested in public policy, and care so much about your community and country.

In terms of advice for you, I would first say "Carry on." We need clear thinking, morally grounded, and common sense people like yourselves contributing to the debates of the public square. And, of course, as Christians, your voice is all the more essential for our commonweal to hear. Keep speaking out, and don't let people shut you down just for being a Christian voicing his opinion on politics. Remember, the separation of church and state is quite different from the separation of religion and society, and of course, our nation's founders would have never thought of the latter.[1] They regarded a worldview derived from the Bible as essential, and indeed, an obvious necessity for a good life and a good country. Now, we're historically quite a ways downstream from the ideas that governed social and political life in the late eighteenth century, but the principles of biblical values and the Judeo-Christian worldview are as relevant and needed as ever, perhaps more so.

And of course, as Christian citizens you have a duty to be active in the life of your community and country. Civic engagement is really an obligation of the believer, and of course any responsible citizen. You can read your Bible and the Constitution, just as you can walk and talk. You can do both at once, and Christians who withdraw from the public square, or regard it as unimportant because it is merely temporal, are making a big mistake. The late Charlie Kirk—a Christian murdered on a college campus while publicly debating faith and values—was a fine model of that dual enterprise.

Now, while I heartily encourage your political engagement, I want to stress that you must remember that politics is not ultimate. The kingdoms of this world—along with their political parties and controversies—will all pass away. There is no salvation in winning

---

1. On this distinction, see Neuhaus, *Naked Public Square*.

policy debates, city council seats, or elections. I hope you will do all three, but keep in mind there is no ultimate fulfillment or salvation there. Only the cross of Christ will lead people to the door of heaven. There is salvation only in Jesus, not in "R" or "D."

The eternal God of the universe transcends political parties and national controversies. He is utterly beyond time, human history, culture, and the local and national controversies of nations. He existed eternally before them, and he will exist eternally after they have passed away. The God and Father of our Lord and Savior Jesus Christ is not a Republican or a Democrat. The God who flung stars into space does not hold a political registration. And he is not an American—or any other nationality. His identity transcends and goes beyond any and all human categories.

Having said that, God is not "value-neutral." He is not indifferent to good and bad; indeed, he is quite the opposite. If the testimony of general revelation—the beauty and order and grandeur of nature and the universe itself—is not enough to convince you of that, just look at a Bible. You don't even have to open it and read it; just look at the cover. It says "Holy Bible." God, the subject of the Bible, is holy. He is of a definite and particular character, a certain attitude, a substantial portion of which is revealed to us in nature, Scripture, and history—both human history and salvation history. Since politics is derived from values, and God is a moral God with values, it follows that not all politics can be equally viable for a human community in his eyes. Government practiced by tyranny, oppression, and murder of dissenters is not pleasing to him. The God of justice has a very keen sense of fairness—indeed a perfect one. All of his many attributes function in perfect cohesion. From Genesis to Revelation, Scripture declares this. Hence unjust human government must be offensive to him. He hates evil.

Now, no government by and of men is perfect, but the pursuit of liberty by a nation is better than the pursuit of violent, dehumanizing, unfair tyranny. The rule of just law is better than the rule of a dictator's whim. While it is true that all human government is going to be imperfect and in some measure corrupt, it does not therefore follow that all forms of human government are equally so flawed.

So while I think it is certainly healthy and important for Christians to recognize that God is not authoring the political platform of their party, it is still critical that Christians realize God is not indifferent to the laws that govern us. I remember I once did an interview with a famous American theologian. He had written many books about contemporary evangelical theology, and he was very keen to remind his readers that God was not a partisan of American politics. I appreciated the points he made during our interview. At one point he asked me if Christians should actively oppose and speak out against abortion. As Christians, in other words, as a proper and appropriate expression of their faith, should Christians openly oppose abortion practice? I said yes, and he rolled his eyes. He thought that such engagement was crass, an unwarranted representation of base political opinion for biblical doctrine. The kingdom of this world and God's kingdom are separate, he affirmed, and the two kingdoms follow a distinct type of logic and government, one human and one divine. To introduce God into local political controversies was to reduce him.

In my view this is a misunderstanding of Christian social ethics. The Bible speaks in an unceasing and holistic moral voice, and how people treat each other individually and socio-politically is of great importance to God. Martin Luther King Jr. understood this so well, which is why the Civil Rights Movement had a rigorous and completely biblical foundation. The language, imagery, and motivation of the movement was utterly and explicitly Judeo-Christian.[2]

So we have a balance here. At once God transcends all human categories and institutions (including political ones), but he is also immanently active in history and concerned about it. He is working for good through his people in the daily affairs of their communities and nations. He is not simply watching from afar the goings-on of people in their lives. He is there with us, working with us, inspiring us, leading us, forgiving us, teaching us, and

---

2. See Branch, *Parting the Waters*.

helping us show his love to those around us. God's transcendence and immanence is applicable to our political lives just as it is to our personal lives.

Lastly, Rick and Brian, I'm glad you're concerned about the harsh and bitter style of political debates in America today. The country is utterly polarized. But don't let that coarse style of politics bother you; that is simply the nature of debate today. Try to be as genial and gentle as you can; that's both a Christian duty and an effective practical strategy. After all, you catch more flies with honey than vinegar. And don't let the polarized, strife-ridden character of debate today cause you to hate those on the other side of issues. That's a danger you must be vigilant against. Try to be charitable towards your political opponents and give them the benefit of the doubt. Assume they are pursuing the good as best they can, according to their lights, just as you are. That may or may not be the case, but start there, and you'll do better connecting with them, and maybe even winning them over to your point of view, if indeed their mind is open.

Politics today generates more heat than light. But in truth, gentlemen, it has always been thus. As you go forward with that awareness and the knowledge that you can make a strong case for your viewpoint, you will do well, and be good stewards of the gift of liberty which is yours.

SONG TO SAVOR:

"All I Once Held Dear" by Robin Mark and Graham Kendrick.[3]

PRAYER:

O God, help me to civilly contend for liberty and goodness, and to bear witness to the values of your word in my time and culture. Help me to always remember politics is not ultimate, and help me to always point people beyond temporal debates, and to your

---

3. Kendrick and Mark, "All I Once Held Dear."

PART II: SOCIAL AND ETHICAL TOPICS

eternal calling upon all of our lives. Give me insight and understanding into my society, the problems it faces, and human nature. Amen.

MEMORIZE:

> I have told you these things, so that in me you might have peace. In this world you will have trouble. But take heart! I have overcome the world. (John 16:33)

SUGGESTED READING:

Dreher, Rod. *Live Not By Lies: A Manual for Christian Dissidents.* New York: Sentinel, 2022.

Lutzer, Erwin W. *We Will Not Be Silenced: Responding Courageously to Our Culture's Assault on Christianity.* Eugene, OR: Harvest House, 2020.

Reno, R. R. *Resurrecting the Idea of a Christian Society.* Nashville: Salem, 2016.

Walsh, Matt. *Church of Cowards: A Wake-Up Call to Complacent Christians.* Washington DC: Regnery, 2022.

Wright, N. T., and Michael F. Bird. *Jesus and the Powers: Christian Political Witness in an Age of Totalitarian Terror and Dysfunctional Democracies.* Grand Rapids: Zondervan, 2024.

9
Abortion

"How does a simple journey of seven inches down the birth canal suddenly transform the essential nature of the fetus from non-person to person?"

—Scott Klusendorf

"Try thinking of . . . the acronym SLED and you'll see [the evils of abortion] even more clearly: Size. How big you are doesn't determine who you are. Level of Development. How developed you are doesn't determine who you are. Environment. Where you are doesn't determine who you are. . . . No amount of size or development or location or dependency makes you more human or less human than another."

—Justin Taylor

"Abortion is the most serious ethical issue that the United States has ever faced."

—R. C. Sproul

Part II: Social and Ethical Topics

From: thebradstetson@gmail.com
To: Susan

Thank you for your letter, Susan. I admire your passion for prenatal life, and your commitment to being a voice for babies in the womb: those who cannot speak for themselves, or tell us what they are thinking and feeling. And I appreciate how overwhelmed you say you feel by the issue, and how you at times feel completely unable to organize your ideas about all the complex themes surrounding abortion as a political and moral topic.

So first, let me directly present to you the case against American abortion practice, and then offer you some advice about pro-life advocacy.

The very nature of abortion advocacy itself contains the basis of its own dissolution. The pro-choice view is that the abortion license must be preserved, irrespective of the nature of prenatal life. But that line of thinking will always come undone, as it suppresses our natural awareness that human beings always and only give birth to other human beings. As the late Illinois congressman Henry Hyde was fond of saying, "No woman has ever given birth to a Golden Retriever."

When a woman is pregnant and overjoyed about it, she talks about "her baby." When the pregnancy is perhaps a surprise or a cause for concern, the baby is called a "fetus." That biological term "fetus" is meant to dehumanize the preborn, and encourage us to not think of the baby as a baby. But contemporary medical advances of ultrasound, fetal therapy, and fetal surgery emphatically demonstrate that prenatal human life is continuous with postnatal human life.

This idea is also just plain common sense. I mean, Susan, if your entire life was being digitally recorded, and we stopped the recording now and began reversing it, what would we see? We would see you one hour ago, a day ago, and a year ago. If we kept going backwards in your life, we would—uninterrupted—see you at the dawn of the new millennium, January 1, 2000, and then still further back, until the day you were born. But the video of your existence and human experience wouldn't stop there. We would see you the day before you were born, and the day before that. We would see you all the way back until "you" began, at the completion of conception, when your father's sperm had fertilized your mother's egg, and that fertilized egg (called a "zygote") successfully implanted in the uterine wall, cells dividing, now called a "blastocyst."

And the growth continues steadily from there. Significantly, the very word "fetus"—Latin for "offspring"—has developmental, not ontological, significance. That is, it denotes a definite and fully established type of being at a certain stage of its existence, not a being which is different in kind from what it will later become. Indeed, it is an objective, genetic reality that even the fertilized human egg—and then the blastocyst, embryo, fetus, and full-term baby—is completely and exclusively human. From conception until death, only water, nourishment, and oxygen are necessary for that human life to flourish on its own terms. As the renowned geneticist Jerome LeJeune succinctly said: "To accept the fact that after fertilization has taken place a new human has come into being is no longer a matter of taste or opinion.... The human nature of the human being from conception to old age is not a metaphysical contention, it is plain experimental evidence."[1]

Eventually, the stress of the national delusion we entered into regarding the inhumanity of the preborn will become too much for our body politic to withstand. Just as on a personal level one lie always leads to other lies more difficult to sustain than the first, so it is socially. The fiction of a baby magically becoming a full human being at birth creates other inhumanities we are loath to bear: gruesome partial-birth abortions, the brutal abandonment of newborns, pregnant women freely drinking alcohol (the leading cause of birth defects), and the refusal of men to accept paternal responsibility ("She could have had an abortion," he reasons).

No social order can encode into law the coarse contempt for nature and organic human relationships that is abortion on demand and expect its fabric to remain intact. The unmatched love

---

1. As quoted in Moreland and Geisler, *Life and Death Debate*, 34.

of a mother for her child has, throughout history, stood as the archetype of personal devotion and selflessness. It is nature's deepest bonding, and culture's highest calling. The abortion license turns mother against child, unleashes a perverse antagonism toward the unexpected or imperfect preborn, and corrupts this most intimate of human affections. All lesser loves are inevitably carried away in the corrosive tide of self-absorption that swells from abortion practice.

When *Roe v. Wade* was overturned by the US Supreme Court in 2022 with the *Dobbs v. Jackson's Women's Health* decision, a kind of national catharsis took place. We came clean about the humanity of the preborn. Now, abortion practice remained unchanged in many states, but with the decision remanded to states' hands, the ethics of abortion became more localized.

So, today, Susan, as an advocate for life it seems to me that where before the approach was macro—a national effort to overturn *Roe*, a case that federalized abortion law and practice—today the approach is more micro. From families to civic organizations to religious organizations, in our localities we must affirm that prenatal life is to be cherished, and we must provide social services (primarily through civic and religious groups) that care for babies once born, easing the hardship on people, women and men, seeking to care for their newborn children. A culture of life like this has already been well underway in communities generally opposed to permissive abortion laws, and as advocates for life we can further support those causes.

Don't doubt yourself, Susan, as you continue to oppose abortion in America. You are fighting true evil. It truly is a hideous practice. Let me talk about this in a more explicit way.

Recall the 2024 presidential campaign. Abortion had been Kamala Harris' favorite issue in the presidential campaign, but as pro-choice advocates have done since *Roe*, she adeptly recited abortion slogans oblivious—willfully or not—to their falsity, and the gory reality of late-term abortions that those slogans conveniently conceal.

Abortion

"A woman can do what she wants with her own body. My body, my choice," she would say. But the baby is clearly not a part of her mother's body. The baby has different DNA than her mother, and may have a different blood type. This cannot be said of any organ or appendage of the mother. The pregnant woman was not born with this baby inside of her, and most probably will not die with this baby inside of her. A baby and her mother are empirically separate human beings. The baby naturally gestates inside her mother, yet the baby and her mother are separate beings, and in time will lead separate human lives. The rhetorical reduction of the preborn human being to maternal property is one means among many to dehumanize the preborn, and justify their disposal.

"Abortion is between a woman and her doctor" is another favorite slogan. Yet, several states allow nurses, nurse-midwives, and physicians' assistants to conduct medication and procedural abortions. No MD necessary. Historically, since even before *Roe*, most legal abortions took place in high-volume clinics, where the woman didn't even meet the doctor until she was already prepped, gowned, and in stirrups. Now, as medication abortions account for slightly more than 60 percent of all such procedures, the deed can be done at home, the prescription drug obtained through a phone call.[2] A far cry, indeed, from the image of a woman and "her physician" carefully consulting and reflecting over the prospective abortion. Encouraging pharmaceutical abortions and surgical abortions often conducted by non-physicians enhances a clinic or abortion provider's bottom line, even if it betrays a favorite saying.

But the deep purpose of such slogans is not really to make a case for public policy; it is rather to provide cover for troubled consciences, to protect oneself (and the public) from seeing with both eyes open the troubling truth: abortion is violent and ugly business, and ends real human life.

The abortion rate today is roughly 1,000,000 per year, with 1 percent (10,000) taking place twenty-one weeks or later into pregnancy.[3] Most of those babies targeted in these "late-term"

---

2. Jones and Friedrich-Karnik, "Medication Abortion."
3. Lague, "Abortion." See the research arm of Planned Parenthood, the

Part II: Social and Ethical Topics

abortions would live if they were allowed to be born. Have you ever wondered what happens in a late-term abortion? Few really know, and most of those who do aren't talking.

But the zeal of true believers occasionally overtakes their sense of the politic, and so Georgia State University sociologist Wendy Simonds, in her remarkable 1996 book *Abortion at Work: Ideology and Practice in a Feminist Clinic*, perhaps unwittingly gave us a crimson tide of revelations through her study of the pseudonymous "Womancare Center" abortion clinic. I urge you, Susan, to read this book to get an understanding of abortion practice. It is extremely unpleasant to read, but it will remind you why you fight against abortion.

The bloody horrors which Simonds—emancipated from moral troubles by what she freely admits is her abortion absolutism—casually relates through interviews with clinic workers are truly stunning.

Here we see the graphic truth always hidden by the fatuous sloganeering of Kamala Harris and her ilk.

For example, one clinic worker whose role was to work in the "sterile room," examining the bodies of preborn human beings who have just been killed by abortion, says:

> It's just—I mean it looks like a baby. It *looks like* a baby. And especially if you get one that comes out, that's not piecemeal. And, you know, I saw this one, and it had its fingers in its mouth . . . it makes me really sad that that had to happen, you know, but it doesn't change my mind. It's just hard. And it makes me just sort of stop and feel sad about it, the whole necessity of it. And also . . . it's very warm when it comes into the sterile room because it's been in the mother's stomach. It feels like flesh, you know.[4]

Another young woman described her response and self-administered reeducation after watching a twenty-one-week abortion: "[When the doctor] takes the forceps and pulls out a foot, you

---

Alan Guttmacher Institute, for further statistics and annual updates.

4. Simonds, *Abortion at Work*, 70–71. Emphasis original.

can see the foot ... [and] I was pretty horrified. And I immediately denied that, and said, you know, 'No, that can't be my reaction. I'm here for the woman,' and just really sort of squashed that down, that what I saw really freaked me out."[5]

Another clinic worker, sometimes assigned to sort through the pieces of dismembered fetuses, explained, "I hate it when people put it together to look like a baby. . . . I hate that. I don't want to look [at] it when it's like that 'cause it's like a broken doll, and that grosses me out."[6] Simonds says many "health workers" (her Orwellian euphemism for abortion center employees) told her they actively avoid looking directly at the face of an aborted baby when they are, in the accepted language of the center, "processing tissue." "Some health workers," Simonds dispassionately notes, "said they wore two pairs of gloves in order to create a barrier of rubber between their hands and the warmth of the tissue and that they tried to use tongs as often as possible, also to keep from having to touch the fetuses."[7]

The tales from this moral crypt go on and on, including the narration of a forced abortion Simonds witnessed which is so revolting and alarming, reading it one feels the impulse to grab a cellphone and call 911.

Though Simonds' unique report is thirty years old, the stark and shocking incongruity between its bloody horror and the antiseptic slogans parroted by Ms. Harris and company is jarring indeed. If the American public looked through windows such as the one Professor Simonds has opened, they would require of Ms. Harris and other pro-choice advocates a more rational and detailed defense of the unspeakably brutal and inhumane industry they deliberately seek to perpetuate and ensconce in our national life.

Susan, advocating for preborn human beings is noble work. It is to stand up for the powerless, and to honor the inherent dignity of human life. These are moral obligations of any good citizen of

---

5. Simonds, *Abortion at Work*, 82.
6. Simonds, *Abortion at Work*, 86.
7. Simonds, *Abortion at Work*, 70–72.

a good republic. The preborn truly are the silent subject in this long national debate. Speaking up for those who themselves cannot will help you find and strengthen your own unique voice as a person, as a citizen of this earthly kingdom, and as a citizen of God's everlasting kingdom—where you will surely find when you get there many human beings created in God's image who were never allowed to be born.

SONG TO SAVOR:

"I Am Not My Own" by Skye Peterson, Ben Shive, Bryan Fowler, and Tom Anderson.[8]

PRAYER:

O God, help me to bear witness in this world to the precious value of preborn human life. Help me to be a sensitive and effective advocate for the surpassing dignity and worth of babies in the womb. Give me great humility as I contend for preborn human life in the public square, and help me to always find ways to help newborn babies and to care for their mothers, whatever their opinions and circumstances.

MEMORIZE:

> For you created my inmost being; you knit me together in my mother's womb. I praise you because I am fearfully and wonderfully made; your works are wonderful, I know that full well. My frame was not hidden from you when I was made in the secret place, when I was woven together in the depths of the earth. Your eyes saw my unformed body; all the days ordained for me were written in your book before one of them came to be. (Ps 139:13–16)

---

8. Getty and Getty, "I Am Not My Own."

SUGGESTED READING:

Beckwith, Francis. *Abortion and the Sanctity of Human Life.* Joplin, MO: College Press, 2000.

———. *Defending Life: A Moral and Legal Case Against Abortion.* Cambridge: Cambridge University Press, 2007.

———. *Politically Correct Death.* Grand Rapids: Baker, 1993.

Klusendorf, Scott. *The Case for Life: Equipping Christians to Engage the Culture.* Wheaton, IL: Crossway, 2009.

Stetson, Brad, ed. *The Silent Subject: Reflections on the Unborn in American Culture.* Westport, CT: Praeger, 1996.

10

Honoring Parents

"If you build a society in which children honor their parents, your society will long survive. And the corollary is: A society in which children do not honor their parents is doomed to self-destruction. In our time, this connection between honoring parents and maintaining civilization is not widely recognized."

—Dennis Prager

"A child who is allowed to be disrespectful to his parents will not have true respect for anyone."

—Billy Graham

"Starting with the generally held Christian belief that God used the Ten Commandments as the foundation of morality, then neglecting or breaking your connection to your parents is an immoral act. Doing the opposite of any one of God's moral laws is by definition immoral."

—Gregory B. Grindstead

Honoring Parents

From: thebradstetson@gmail.com
To: Steve

Your question is a great one, Steve; I'm so glad you asked it. As you note, it seems to me there is an epidemic of young people "canceling" their parents and refusing to speak to them. For parents, losing contact with their children is devastating, to say the least. It is unspeakably hurtful to them, and oftentimes irrational and inexplicable from the parents' point of view.[1] I've heard of children never speaking to their parents again because their parents voted for Trump, or the parents oppose transsexual surgery for minors, or because the parents expressed displeasure at the choice of a boyfriend. The reasons are legion, and wrong. When I think about this topic, I'm reminded of the old saying: "We do the devil's work for him, and he doesn't even say thank you." Forsaking parents truly is a demonic practice.

Now, of course, there are those rare circumstances where it simply may not be possible for a child to continue a relationship with their parents. I'm thinking specifically of physical and sexual abuse that happened during childhood, and other such profoundly wrong and directly harmful treatment. But that is not the nature of the epidemic today. It is rather children—nearly grown or grown—feeling empowered by rage or a misguided moral sense, and on that basis excluding parents from their lives. Remember the commandment in Exod 20 does not have a time limit on it. It's not "honor your mother and father until they are seventy years old, or until you are thirty." It's permanent. We are to respect them and treat them decently always. Notably, the commandment isn't to "love" your parents. Of course we usually do love our parents, but honoring them, respecting them, and tolerating their idiosyncrasies does not necessarily entail "love" in the intimate emotional sense.

The great Jewish writer Dennis Prager is fond of telling a story about his own father that seems to me to illustrate very well the sentiment behind "honoring" our mother and father. Prager

1. For insightful discussion, see Prager, "What's Causing Pandemic."

grew up in Brooklyn, New York, in the middle of the twentieth century. His father was an accountant, I think, and every day his father would come home from a hard day's work, and sit with the family at the dinner table. Each night, around the same time, Dennis' grandmother—his father's mother—would call up his father on the phone. Each night was the same routine. He would answer the phone with "Hi Ma," and the elderly woman would then begin a litany of complaints. She would complain about everything, from her aches and pains to relatives living and dead. Dennis' father would simply place the receiver of the old phone down on the table, and periodically speak into it, "Yes, Ma, yes, Ma." He allowed his mother to call and vent each evening, even though he was no doubt tired after work, wanted to enjoy his meal, or perhaps had something important to say to one of his family members. But he politely let his mother talk, and then he would say goodbye, only to have the ritual repeat itself the next night. It went on for years. Dennis' father was a religious Jew, and felt his obligation to his mother required this selfless patience and deference. A far cry, indeed, from how many self-regarding adult children might react today to such phone calls.

So Steve, you are a young adult now, and you are starting to see that your parents are imperfect people too, facing a lot of the challenges in life that you face, or one day will. In time you will see your mom and dad more and more like regular people, burdened with all the economic, emotional, and personal stresses of life. As we age they become less superhuman and more human in our eyes. Hopefully your appreciation of them will grow, and you will find yourself becoming increasingly grateful for the sacrifices they made for you. And that knowledge of how they lived, and that gratitude for what they accomplished, will empower you when you yourself become a father and face that great challenge. What kind of father will you be?

That's a good question, and one that I think every young man should ask himself. I mean, we plan ahead for things that are important in our lives, and what could be more important than being responsible for bringing up a child one day?

Lastly, Steve, let me say a word about forgiveness. When we become adults, if not sooner, we must forgive our parents for their mistakes. Every parent makes mistakes raising their children, and children are good at remembering those mistakes. But don't hold those mistakes against your parents, forgive them—and know that they were doing their best as flawed, imperfect human beings. That attitude will benefit you so much going forward, and it will liberate you from bitterness and a crippling resentment that can only be a destructive force in your life. All of us flawed and troubled human beings are "companions in shipwreck," so to speak, and so may mercy be our common byword.

SONG TO SAVOR:

"Good Good Father" by Chris Tomlin.[2]

PRAYER:

O God, lead me to always remember to honor my parents, and to be grateful for the sacrifices they made for me. Empower me, Lord, to forgive them of their shortcomings and imperfections, and help me to learn from their lives, to encourage them in their own lives, and honor their legacy in this world. Amen.

MEMORIZE:

> Honor your father and your mother, so that you may live long in the land the Lord your God is giving you. (Exod 20:12)

SUGGESTED READING:

Fields, Leslie Leyland, and Jill Hubbard. *Forgiving Our Fathers and Mothers: Finding Freedom from Hurt and Hate.* Nashville: Thomas Nelson, 2014.

2. Tomlin, "Good, Good Father."

Part II: Social and Ethical Topics

Grimstead, Gregory B. *The Hidden Promise, Honoring Your Parents: A Christian Perspective on How, Why and When to Honor Your Parents*. Scotts Valley, CA: CreateSpace, 2014.

Stanley, Charles. *5 Things to Pray for Your Parents: Prayers That Change Things for an Older Generation*. Charlotte, NC: Good Book, 2012.

Stoop, David. *Forgiving Our Parents, Forgiving Ourselves: The Definitive Guide*. Grand Rapids: Fleming Revell, 2011.

Yep, Jeanette, et al., eds. *Following Jesus Without Dishonoring Your Parents*. Downers Grove, IL: InterVarsity, 1998.

11

Dating and Marriage

"Love . . . is not merely a feeling. It is a deep unity, maintained by the will and deliberately strengthened by habit; reinforced by (in Christian marriages) the grace which both partners ask, and receive, from God. They can have this love for each other even at those moments when they do not like each other; as you love yourself even when you do not like yourself."

—C. S. Lewis

"A happy marriage is the union of two good forgivers."

—Ruth Graham

"Nothing will bring two hearts closer together than two hearts that are after the heart of God."

—Adam Cappa

From: thebradstetson@gmail.com
To: Anna

Thank you for your note, Anna, and of course you raise the central question on the minds of most young men and women, certainly

Christian ones: Should I get married, and how will I know who to marry? The answer is "Yes" and "Yes." Let me explain.

Remember the creation story. Each day after God created, he blessed his creation by saying, "It was good." But when it came to the man, Adam, his commentary was, "It is not good that man should be alone" (Gen 2:18). Human persons, men and women, are usually happier with partners, and the commitment that is marriage is the best context for lifelong partnership. Marriage can be a difficult enterprise for people, to be sure. But aspiring to a meaningful and satisfying and happy marriage is one of the great goals of life.

Perhaps the more challenging question is not "Should I get married?" but "Who should I marry, and how will I know?" When I answered the "who" question with "Yes" earlier, what I meant was you will know, intuitively and in your heart, when you have met and come to know someone you want to be a life-partner. Oftentimes, though not always, love can create a literally "buzzed" or "dazed" feeling. The phrases "lovestruck," "punch-drunk love," or "lovesick" all reflect this common knowledge. So in many instances, a person may experience this kind of somatic or bodily knowledge that they are in love, and that the one who is the object of their love is more than just a passing interest.

But certainly that is only a generalization, and it must not be the only criterion. The old saying, "Men learn to love who they are attracted to, and women learn to be attracted to who they love," has some currency. Sometimes love grows organically, or naturally, as you spend time with someone and get to know them.

And this process of getting to know someone is very, very important, irrespective of what first attracted you to them. And of course, as a Christian, you require your spouse to share your faith and much of your values. Those are biblical necessities.

I think the old-fashioned two-year rule is a very good one, although these days, especially for people over, say, thirty years old, one might shorten it to the year-and-a-half rule. This time span, whatever it may be exactly, is very important. Because it is time—and the many experiences with a person that you have over time—that allows you to really get to know another person. It is vital that you see your prospective mate in many different circumstances and situations. What is he like when he is happy or sad? How does he respond to disappointment, frustration, insults, and success? What is he like around his friends? How does he treat waiters and service workers? How does he treat his parents and siblings? You have to see him in these many postures of life in order to gain an understanding of his personality and character. Presumably he's on his best behavior around you, but you need to get a picture of who he is amid all the challenges of contemporary life. Pray that God will speak to your heart about him, and that you will come to accurately know his mind and heart.

Of course this includes his social media. You don't have to stalk him on the internet, but do some searching. Go to the Google box and type his name in, in quotes, for example, "Brad Stetson." Then after his name add another word, such as the name of his city, or place of work, or college name. See what you see. Presumably you already have access to his Instagram or Facebook or TikTok page or other new media. Check that too. Sometimes you will find out things you never could have imagined.

I remember when I was a faculty member at a university. We had to hire a new faculty member, and I was on the search committee. So we conducted a big worldwide search over many months. We received many outstanding applications. After a period of review we invited just three people, out of several dozen, to come for an interview. We talked in person to each of these three candidates, each one an outstanding historian, excellent in their field of specialty. But there was one candidate who stood out, head and shoulders above the rest. He was simply brilliant, and highly accomplished. So we had one final faculty meeting amongst ourselves, and decided that we would offer this individual—let's call him "Bill"—the position.

So that night, I went home and thought about this man. I knew all about his professional work, but I didn't know much else about him. So I Googled him, and it was a good thing I did!

Part II: Social and Ethical Topics

It turns out that some years ago back in his hometown—a medium-sized city with a college at which he taught—he had been embroiled in an intense controversy over Holocaust denial. Bill had delivered a lecture at the college, followed up by an op-ed he wrote in the local paper and a few letters to the editor of that paper, all defending his view that the Holocaust was mostly a made-up, fabricated, pseudo-historical event. His arguments were odd and puzzling, and his evidence ridiculous and utterly unconvincing. It wasn't intellectually serious, yet he was certainly serious about it, for whatever reasons. At any rate, for someone seeking to become a history professor at a mainstream university—or any university worth the name—this was a deal-breaker. I emailed the chair of the department the information I'd found, the faculty met the next day, and we settled on a different candidate for the job.

So, it goes to show you that people are not always what they seem, and you have to dig deep, experientially and otherwise, before you can be confident you know someone. For young people, or anyone I should think, deliberating about marriage, "take your time" has got to be sound advice. Whether it's two years or a little shorter or longer, getting the big picture of somebody—seeing them through a "macroscope," if you will—is vital.

Also, although parents and family members are not infallible guides in these matters, definitely have him meet your parents and relatives. They know you well (even if you don't think so), and they probably have some wisdom gained through the years, so their point of view is important to get. The old dictum, "You marry the family," is pretty true, I think. So, when you think the time is right, definitely bring him over to meet the parents. It's a big step.

Well, Anna, you're smart to be serious about these matters, because they are inherently serious. I can't think of any life experience that can enrich your overall life and sense of wellbeing more than a solid, stable, and happy marriage.

And remember as you think about these matters, be sure to be the kind of person you yourself would like to marry. That is, live the faith and values you profess. Demonstrate the moral judgment you want to see in others, including prospective spouses. Be an excellent woman who puts Jesus first in her life, and you will discover that you attract like-minded men.

And yet, always be realistic. Remember, you're marrying a human being, not a demigod. He will be flawed and fallible in all the regular ways. The old maxim "The perfect is the enemy of the good" is especially relevant here. Your prospective spouse doesn't have to be perfect in order to be good. And for that matter, neither do you.

SONG TO SAVOR:

"It's Always Been You" by Phil Wickham.[1]

PRAYER:

O God, give me insight and discernment in choosing a spouse, and in becoming the kind of person who would be a good spouse. Help me to exemplify the virtues I desire in others, and lead me to grow in the grace and knowledge of Jesus Christ. I pray he would increase within me, and I would decrease. May your will be done in my life. Amen.

MEMORIZE:

> Love is patient, love is kind. It does not envy, it does not boast, it is not proud. It does not dishonor others, it is not self-seeking, it is not easily angered, it keeps no record of wrongs. Love does not delight in evil but rejoices with the truth. It always protects, always trusts, always hopes, always perseveres. (1 Cor 13:4–7)

---

1. Wickham, "It's Always Been You."

PART II: SOCIAL AND ETHICAL TOPICS

SUGGESTED READING:

Cloud, Henry, and John Townsend. *Boundaries in Dating: How Healthy Choices Grow Healthy Relationships*. Grand Rapids: Zondervan, 2000.

Keller, Timothy, and Kathy Keller. *The Meaning of Marriage: Facing the Complexities of Commitment with the Wisdom of God*. New York: Penguin, 2013.

Thomas, Gary L. *Sacred Marriage: What if God Designed Marriage to Make Us Holy More Than to Make Us Happy?* Grand Rapids: Zondervan, 2015.

———. *The Sacred Search: What if It's Not About Who You Marry, But Why?* Colorado Springs, CO: David C. Cook, 2013.

Trobisch, Walter. *I Married You*. North Collins, NY: Quiet Waters, 1971.

12

Sex and Sexuality

"I fear many of us have become numb to the poison we are drinking. When it comes to sexual immorality, sin looks normal, righteousness looks very strange, and [Christians] look a lot like everybody else."

—Kevin DeYoung

"No sin that a person commits has more built-in pitfalls, problems and destructiveness than sexual sin. It has broken more marriages, shattered more homes, caused more heartache and disease, and destroyed more lives than alcohol and drugs combined. It causes lying, stealing, cheating and killing, as well as bitterness, hatred, slander, gossip and unforgiveness."

—John MacArthur

"It would seem that Our Lord finds our desires not too strong, but too weak. We are half-hearted creatures, fooling about with drink and sex and ambition when infinite joy is offered us, like an ignorant child who wants to go on making mud pies in a slum because he cannot imagine what is meant by the offer of a holiday at the sea. We are far too easily pleased."

—C. S. Lewis

Part II: Social and Ethical Topics

From: thebradstetson@gmail.com
To: Tom and Michelle

Thank you both for writing, and congratulations on your engagement! You mentioned you are a little apprehensive that because you're getting married before your senior year of college, you'll both be some of the very few married students on campus. But don't worry about that. If anything, the other students will be jealous that you have found a life-partner so young.

I also think you are quite right to recognize the wide separation between the traditional Christian ethic of sexuality and the common assumptions in American culture today about what's permissible. It's easy to see that there's a big difference, of course, but reflecting on the forces generating and superintending this gulf is worthwhile.

First, though, I like to stress that there is perhaps no other area of life that consistently causes so much pain and suffering to human beings than does sex and sexuality. So much so, it may well not be an exaggeration to say that nearly everyone has experienced some kind of suffering in this area. Given this ubiquity, one would think there is much literature about the proper understanding of human sexuality and the myriad problems with the contemporary ethic. But the writing on the topic is not commensurate with the hardship it causes in human life.

Sex is like a river. If it flows consistently between its banks, it is a positive and nourishing presence in its environment. It gives life and adds beauty to everything around it. However, if it overflows its boundaries and floods the surrounding areas, it causes chaos, hardship, and even destruction. Indeed, in nature, the flood is one of the most damaging of catastrophes. A serious flood can even wipe out an entire city. So it is all the more appropriate, given sex's destructive force, to spend some time thinking about sexual ethics.

At the outset, of course, we can say that as Christians we have a standard, a north star. That is, we have a fixed and constant guide to the proper expression of human sexuality, and that is Scripture.

It may not be in wide use today, it may not be reflected in media and entertainment, and it may not be taught in schools, but that's irrelevant. We don't decide what's right based on what's widely accepted. Scripture's authority for Christians is not dependent on any of those things. The guide we have is validated not because of its cultural authority (which often seems small), not because of its ease, and not because of its recommendation by experts, but because it is to us God's word. And, in truth, it has stood the test of time. For all the revilement "old-school" or "old-fashioned" ethics get, the outcome they produce in human experience stacks up very well against its competitors.

The proper expression of human sexuality is found within the boundaries of traditional heterosexual marriage. Full stop. If that seems harsh or unenlightened, well that's a testimony to the extent of our unhealthy outlook on sex today. I know, of course, that this biblical ethic may seem unattainable to you today, or utterly impractical. But those are the lies of our time. It can be done, and if a person develops the right habits as they spiritually and personally mature, then it will be much easier for them to meet this biblical standard.

Now, I don't want to seem clueless and out of touch. I know full well we live in a pornographic society, literally saturated with sex and sexual images. From morning 'til night, from smartphones to computers to television, sexual images of all kinds surround us. David's and Job's ancient wisdom to guard our hearts and be careful what we look at is all the more necessary for us today. (See Ps 101:3 and Job 31:1.) After all, the eyes are the gateway to the heart.

And given this hyper-sexualized culture, it is easy for someone to develop bad or unhelpful habits, and to offend God. When we do this, we must go to the cross and sincerely seek his forgiveness and the resolve to change. And if we must do this repeatedly, then indeed we must. Never give up, never believe that you can't honor God in this central area of life, because that is simply a lie.

And the truth is, Tom and Michelle, for a lot of people, especially men, the pursuit of sexual activity is goal number one. It is their top priority in life, even if they don't frankly acknowledge that to themselves. Anything that gets in the way of that, like following Jesus and living the gospel, has got to go.

For a lot of young people living in contemporary Western society, the Christian ethic is so far away, it seems so unattainable, they don't even want to try. Of course, they err by not first realizing that once they are born again their passions and their aspirations will reflect the priorities of the kingdom of God, and they will have the Holy Spirit within them to empower them to honor God.

I remember an experience I had in college. It was about forty-five years ago, but it pictured in little the attitude of so many young men still today. I had a religion class, I think it was a class in New Testament history, and it was a general education class. It met a history requirement for an undergraduate degree. The professor was a nice man, but he didn't believe a word of the New Testament; to him it was like reading Homer or Plato, interesting but not inspired or inspiring. He knew, of course, Christians would be drawn to his class, and he was always very patient and respectful to Christian students who asked questions or spoke up about their faith.

I did that one day in class, and after the bell I was standing at the bike racks with the student in class who sat next to me. Let's say his name was Austin. Austin commented to me that the discussion in class was interesting, but he felt that at age twenty-one, the world was just too brimming with excitement and possibilities for him to think about following Jesus. At that moment, a female student, who had parked her bike near ours, began to get up on to the seat of her bicycle. Her skirt was short, and as she lifted her leg to get on the seat, well, Austin and I got a clear look at her underwear. He chuckled and looked at me and said, with gleeful conviction, "You see? That's why I can't be a Christian!"

Austin didn't understand the gospel, what it meant to be born again, or how empty and unfulfilling the life he wanted would be for him. But his attitude certainly captures the culture he imbibed.

For Christians to have a clear understanding of sex and human sexuality in our time, I would like to offer eight brief principles to keep in mind that will help ground and orient our thinking in this critical area.

First, remember, as I said earlier, Scripture only presents one appropriate course for believers. One husband, one wife, together in a commitment before God, is the biblical context for a sexual relationship. Everything else, however exalted by the spirit of our age or our own vaunted preferences, is morally wrong. By God's grace we can accept this, and live this. In fact, it is what is best for us, and it is not second best to some other alternative.

Second, though this is the case, God's love for everyone is a constant. No matter what anyone has done, no matter when they did it, God still loves them and wants their heart to find its rest in him. Just like the father of the prodigal son who was always keeping a lookout in the distance so he could see the moment his lost son turned his eyes toward him, God's arms are always open to us (Luke 15:11–32). His love for us is unwavering, even if we don't perceive it.

Third, remember that men and women are complementary, and need one another. Genesis chapter two makes that clear, and male and female each reflect the image of God in their own way. Taken together, in marriage, they convey God's image uniquely, and fulfill their own humanity uniquely. This is an important reason for marriage, as is procreation. Every child deserves a loving, decent, responsible mother and father, and the commitment of marriage is the time-tested, best method to achieve that condition.[1]

Fourth, it's helpful to remember that every human being has, because of our fallen condition, a disordered sexuality. Sometimes this natural state is compounded by bad habits we've developed, but every person, man or woman, is saddled with some aspect in our sexual drive that seeks to lead us away from God. Note, of course, being tempted is not sinning, and God by his Spirit always empowers us to resist temptation and defeat (1 Cor 10:13). This is a battle every man faces, and every woman too.

Fifth, remember that sexual intimacy is not an automatic right that everyone will enjoy. Some people just never develop

---

1. For further discussion along these lines, see Stanton, "Ten Things."

their sexuality, or they never get married wherein they can express their sexuality. This kind of disappointment is simply a fact of life. Yet, in our sexually confused time, such a disappointment is sometimes regarded as intolerable, and even unjust. For example, over the last few years the "incel" culture has arisen, which takes a rage-filled approach to sexual disappointment. Sometimes this pathological view results in misogyny or even murder. It is, of course, a perspective Christians must absolutely avoid.

Sixth, in our sexually obsessed times, remember that your personal identity or value does not lie in sex or your sexuality. You are much more than sexual desires, and your identity is far deeper and more complex than sexuality. Sex is one dimension of your humanity, but only one. You bear the image of God, you are a member of the human community, and you have myriad interests and capacities that go far beyond the sexual. The contemporary reduction of a person to his or her sexuality is in fact dehumanizing, and a great misunderstanding of the fullness of human life.

Seventh, as a Christian living in a sexually disordered society, resist its cues to you regarding sex. Do not cultivate or nurture sexual desire. This fantasization of sex and sexual desire is central to popular culture and so much media and entertainment. It's fine to naturally feel sexual desire, to have sexual drives, but we don't need to cultivate it and feed it with thoughts, images, and imaginations. It's strong enough on its own, we don't need to dwell and brood upon it. The psychologization of sex today, locating it at the center of who we are and all we do and think, is a part of our contemporary sexual disorder. Freud's work lives on in our society so devoted to all things sexual.

Lastly, Tom and Michelle, remember God's mercy. He knows the social context and the historical era in which we live, and his judgment of us is always tempered with his mercy and wisdom. He knows our culture is sexually sick, and he knows the influences—familial, behavioral, ideological—that we were subjected to growing up. He knows that we may have been victimized as children. His understanding of us, and what we do and think, is shaped by his omniscient and loving heart. So he knows us; he always knows what we are thinking and feeling, no matter the area of life, and his compassion and forgiveness towards us is abundant, and it never wanes. He loves us with a love that transcends what we can even begin to truly understand, it is so great. He wants the best for us. He wants us to walk with him, to honor him, and to find ourselves in his loving heart. He knows that is best for us.

So, Tom and Michelle, I wish you well in your lives together, and in all God will do through the family that by his grace and goodness may be yours. May your union be a great and inspiring example to those around you. How fortunate you are to have found each other in this world!

SONG TO SAVOR:

"At the Cross" by Brian Doerksen.[2]

PRAYER:

O God, help me to truly love everyone in my life, including my spouse. Give me a proper and rightly ordered understanding of human sexuality, and help me to help others who have been harmed or injured by their experiences in this area. Give me compassion for others, and help me to stand for the truth about human sexuality in my community and society.

MEMORIZE:

> Do not love the world or anything in the world. . . . For everything in the world—the lust of the flesh, the lust of the eyes, and the pride of life—comes not from the Father but from the world. The world and its desires pass away, but whoever does the will of God lives forever. (1 John 2:15–17)

2. Doerksen, "At the Cross."

PART II: SOCIAL AND ETHICAL TOPICS

SUGGESTED READING:

Anderson, Neil T. *Winning the Battle Within: Realistic Steps to Overcoming Sexual Strongholds.* Eugene, OR: Harvest House, 2008.

Arterburn, Stephen, and Fred Stoeker. *Every Young Man's Battle: Strategies for Victory in the Real World of Sexual Temptation.* Colorado Springs, CO: Waterbrook, 2002.

Boa, Andrew A. *Redeemed Sexuality: Healing and Transformation in Community.* Downers Grove, IL: InterVarsity, 2017.

Pearcey, Nancy R. *Love Thy Body: Answering Hard Questions About Life and Sexuality.* Grand Rapids: Baker, 2018.

Slattery, Juli. *Rethinking Sexuality: God's Design and Why It Matters.* Colorado Springs, CO: Multnomah, 2018.

13

Alcohol and Drugs

"Idolatry . . . includes anything on which we set our affections and indulge as an excessive and sinful attachment. . . . Idolatry includes anything we worship: the lust for pleasure, respect, love, power, control, or freedom from pain. Furthermore, the problem is not outside of us, located in a liquor store or on the Internet; the problem is within us. Alcohol and drugs are essentially satisfiers of deeper idols. The problem is not with the idolatrous substance; it is the false worship of the heart."

—EDWARD WELCH

"One of the marks of a certain type of bad man is that he cannot give up a thing himself without wanting everyone else to give it up. That is not the Christian way. An individual Christian may see fit to give up all sorts of things for special reasons—marriage, or meat, or beer, or the cinema; but the moment he starts saying the things are bad in themselves, or looking down his nose at other people who do use them, he has taken the wrong turning."

—C. S. LEWIS

"A biblical approach to change focuses on someone other than ourselves. Change starts, proceeds, and ends with Jesus. We look to Jesus and away from ourselves."

—Edward Welch

From: thebradstetson@gmail.com
To: James

I agree with you, James, alcohol abuse is a huge issue for young adults, including Christians. The drinking culture on college campuses and among young adults has continued unabated for years. It's almost as though college-aged students feel some sort of perverse obligation to drink.

I remember when I taught at a university in a college town. I went to a Rite-Aid drugstore, rather late at night, about 11 p.m. It was near the campus. As I stood in line to buy my item, I saw in front of me a small group of young women, about college-aged. They dressed like students from the school, and I assumed that's what they were. They were certainly the right age. I noticed each one of them had a large bottle of Jack Daniels whiskey. They got up to the cashier, produced their identification to prove they were twenty-one, and they made their purchase. They seemed so nonchalant yet also reluctant about this, and so oblivious to the harm it could do them. They seemed to feel compelled to obtain this alcohol. I was about to say to them, "The answers to your problems are not at the bottom of that bottle," but they were gone before I gathered the forthrightness to do so. But I remember them, and the sadness they exhibited, and the sense that they were doing something they thought they were supposed to do, not something they really wanted to do, not something they were happy about doing.

I want to stress, James, how dangerous alcohol is. It's an underrated threat to college students, and people in general. The damage caused by alcohol is immense. The hurtful words spoken while under the influence, the bad behavioral decisions, the harm caused by driving drunk—the toll is simply staggering. Just this week in my city five high-school-aged students died when the car being driven by one of them (who was drunk) hit a tree.

Why do so many people drink to excess? The reasons are as diverse as the lives of each one of those people. We have become accustomed to taking refuge in substances to evade our problems (or so we think) by numbing ourselves. I think if young adults like yourself could get a fresh look at the havoc wrought by alcohol it might penetrate the social authority inclining people to drink. I used to ask students in the classes I taught if they were morally obligated to drink alcohol at campus parties. They always hesitated a bit when I framed the question that way, and then they acknowledged that they were not obligated to drink. They were often quick to add that they wanted to, it was their free choice, but usually their assertions of liberty struck me as a case of protesting too much. They weren't really happy about that choice, and often I think they wished drinking didn't seem socially *de riguer.*

Imagine if during orientation for incoming university students, the emphasis wasn't on "consent" or "choice" but on the real threat alcohol consumption is to one's future. A drunk driving citation costs thousands of dollars and is a serious detriment to one's credibility; a sexual assault charge can easily result from an encounter where one or both of the participants are inebriated; the harm one can cause or sustain through a drunk driving accident is as serious as life or death itself. I can't think of any other conduct so widely accepted that carries with it so many outsized and utterly serious dangers.

So, James, I think it is best in these years of your young adulthood to just stay away from liquor. You're not really missing anything important, and you could be sparing yourself profound regret.

With respect to drug use, like marijuana, I can only say there are some avenues we simply should just not go down. I know it's now legal in many jurisdictions, and it is the subject of a lot of humor in media. And of course the general social attitude is it's "no big deal." But I think those attitudes are misguided, and a real danger lurks behind that cultural permission.

Part II: Social and Ethical Topics

Not far from my house there is a section of town called "El Modena." It is a known gang neighborhood, even though so much of regular daily life transpires there too. Once I was driving around, and curious about several of the small streets that sprouted off the main boulevard in El Modena. I didn't know what lay down those streets, but I'd always wondered. I'd been driving by them for years. After all, I had never seen much of the reputed gang activity in this neighborhood, so close to my own. So, heeding my curiosity, I drove down one of those narrow streets, lined with old cars and overgrown willow trees.

I immediately regretted my decision. The street quickly ended in a cul-de-sac, and as I reached the dead end, I was in the midst of nearly a dozen young men—tattooed and bald—just standing at the head of the cul-de-sac and leaning up against the fences in the front yards of the small homes there. They stared at me with un-welcoming eyes and a look that said, "You shouldn't have come here." I executed the quickest three-point U-turn of my life and quickly drove away.

No harm came to me because of my errant turn, but I thought to myself, "I didn't need to do that. I didn't need to know what lay down that street, and I could have been harmed." So it is with drugs and alcohol. You don't have to know what they will do to you; you don't need to go there. There are some turns we best not make. The literature documenting the harm of marijuana is rapidly proliferating, and now with its legalization widespread, an awareness of the dangers it poses is all the more important.[1]

At the very least, everyone—especially young adults—should know that marijuana use impedes emotional and psychological development and maturity. It attenuates motivation and an urgent awareness of life's importance, and it habituates us to taking refuge in its effects rather than facing the circumstances and challenges of life. And in truth, James, there's a lot of propaganda surrounding marijuana use. It persists in being seen as cool and "chill," and anyone resisting it as uptight, uncool, and a dud. Well, just because not everyone is harmed by it every time they use it, that doesn't mean

---

1. Volkow et al., "Adverse Health Effects."

it's a harmless choice. It's addictive, and every addiction subtracts from our liberty, and dehumanizes us.

And, in truth, when it comes to marijuana at least, we may not be the only ones harmed. I had a childhood friend, let's call him "Steven." We grew up together. In his late teens, nearing the end of high school, he experienced some disappointments in life. He struggled in school, his parents divorced, he was socially awkward. He began to smoke marijuana. It was the tenth grade when he started, and it quickly became known around school and the neighborhood that Steven was smoking a lot of pot, and that he could even sell you some, if you asked. He was remarkably open about it. In fact, I think it became a point of pride to him that he was the guy who smoked a lot of pot, and could get you some if you wanted. This went on for a few years, until he was about age twenty-three. Then, his mother caught him with a trash bag full of marijuana in his bedroom. He was in big trouble. I didn't see him for a long time. Then, off and on for the next ten years or so, I'd run into him around town, and he seemed to be doing fine. He told me he'd gotten married, and his wife was pregnant with a daughter. I congratulated him, and then the next time I saw him, about five years later, I asked him how his child was. His response was far from the ebullient, proud father you would expect. He was subdued, and sheepish. He said his daughter was OK, but was really struggling in school. I said she'd grow out of it and come around, but he seemed to suspect otherwise. Sure enough, after several years, when she was high-school aged, I found out she had severe learning disabilities, a reduced IQ, and trouble communicating with people. Her brain didn't process information in a typical way, and she attended a local school for students with various special needs. I inferred from all this that Steven, due to his extremely heavy and sustained consumption of marijuana as a young man, had damaged his sperm, and now his daughter paid the price every day of her life.[2] So, James, sometimes our bad choices in this regard can have permanent harmful effects on others, including family.

---

2. The literature on this is vast and proliferating; see for example Duke Health, "Impact of Paternal Marijuana Exposure."

Part II: Social and Ethical Topics

I remember when I worked as a chaplain at Riverside County Jail in Riverside, California. It was an enormous facility, with dozens and dozens of men housed in "tanks." These were large rooms overcrowded with prisoners. The jail was segregated by race, as all prisons are, so a separate tank each held the whites, the blacks, the Hispanics.

But when it came time for chapel, a mix of races attended. I would have a smaller room of about twenty to thirty men sitting on benches for the chapel service. I always had a question-and-answer session as a part of each chapel, and inevitably, as the men would talk, one common problem emerged: drugs. I would estimate, conservatively, that 75 percent of the inmates were there for a conviction on drug use or drug sales, or both. And those men who were there for a more violent felony, they usually committed that crime while under the influence of drugs and alcohol. Their lives were full of regret and pain, and a deep sense of sadness and hopelessness. And drug use played a big role in taking them to that lost place.

So James, if at this young age you can decide that life is interesting enough on its own terms, and you can resolve to avoid alcohol and drugs, you will gain a mile in the Christian walk. Remember Christian discipleship is, in the words of Eugene Peterson, "a long obedience in the same direction."[3] As we walk with him day by day, day in and day out, we learn what it means to be his student, and to process and understand our daily lives under his love and lordship. He will make a way for us, as we commit ourselves to him.

SONG TO SAVOR:

"Christ Is Lower Still" by Matt Maher, Kate Bluett, Isaac Wardell, and Doe Jones.[4]

---

3. See Peterson's classic book, *Long Obedience in the Same Direction*.
4. The Porter's Gate, "Christ Is Lower Still."

PRAYER:

O Lord, I know you receive me as I am, with my addictions, shortcomings, sins, and failures. I thank you for your love and mercy and forgiveness. I pray that you would take me up in your arms, hold me, and heal me. Draw me nearer and nearer to you, and I pray my addictions and ugly habits would be crowded out of me by my love for you, devotion to you, and overwhelming desire to honor you. By your Holy Spirit conform me to the image of Jesus Christ. Amen.

MEMORIZE:

> Do you not know that your bodies are temples of the Holy Spirit, who is in you, whom you have received from God? You are not your own; you were bought at a price. Therefore honor God with your bodies. (1 Cor 6:19–20)

SUGGESTED READING:

Anderson, Neil T., et al. *Freedom From Addiction*. Ventura, CA: Regal, 1996.

Arterburn, Stephen, and David Stoop. *Understanding and Loving a Person with Alcohol and Drug Addiction*. Colorado Springs, CO: David C. Cook, 2018.

Northrup, Lanier T. *When God Calls You to Recovery: Using the Lord's Strength to Break and Destroy Addiction*. Tulsa, OK: Trilogy Christian, 2020.

Shaw, Mark E. *The Heart of Addiction*. Bemidji, MN: Focus, 2008.

Welch, Edward T. *Addictions: A Banquet in the Grave*. Phillipsburg, NJ: P & R, 2001.

14

Television and Media

"Christians should not allow entertainment to define their understanding of happiness, romance, modesty, masculinity, success, fulfillment, justice, or anything else. The Word and the Spirit should shape our worldview, not Hollywood. Sadly, however, many Christians today are more affected by the movies they watch than the sermons they hear."

—John MacArthur

"Television encourages passivity and diminishes creativity. And it disrupts natural family life. Worst of all, it induces what has been called 'the television trance.' It has not merely blurred the distinctions between the real and unreal for steady viewers, but by doing so it has dulled their sensitivities to real events."

—Derek Bingham

"People who have [television] sets seem to do nothing but go into a huddle over them every evening of their lives, instead of being out walking, or in their gardens. And of course, like all things which begin as luxuries, they end up being necessities."

—C. S. Lewis

Television and Media

From: thebradstetson@gmail.com
To: Maria

Yes, of course, Maria, you're right that Christians should spend much more time thinking about their consumption of television and media. What are we watching? What could be its effects and influences upon us? Are these images or this story helpful to me as a person, or are they harmful?

We need to be conscious of our media consumption, and not mindless. Sometimes, I think, we regard TV, radio, podcasts, and other media consumption as things that happen to us, rather than as choices we deliberately make. Perhaps the most helpful ideas I can express to you, Maria, are based on my own consumption of media, which I admit has been prodigious.

First, with respect to television news. In my home growing up the "news" was always on; my parents were true newshounds. It's a habit that persisted my whole life. Only in the last twenty years or so have I started to realize how emotionally manipulative and harmful TV news can be. "If it bleeds it leads" has been the mantra of local news across media markets in the US for years, but it's a harmful theme. Night after night, the "murder report," as I came to call it, intoned episodes of incomprehensible human suffering and misery brought on by equally incomprehensible acts of human evil—all in one-minute packages, with rarely any follow-up on the suffering of the poor souls displayed for our horror and amusement.

I realized that these announcements of brutal violence, night after night, were harming and depressing me. Paradoxically, though, it did lead me to begin studying the sociology and psychology of homicide victims' families, and how they coped. This led me to publish two books on the subject.[1] But the mind-numbing effect of hearing about epic human suffering, and lives and families ruined every night, was harmful to me.

I came to realize this terrible effect when I asked myself a simple question: Did I need to hear this? *Why are you telling me*

---

1. Stetson, *Living Victims, Stolen Lives*, and Stetson, *Choosing to Survive*.

Part II: Social and Ethical Topics

this? I would sometimes ask out loud to the newscast anchor. I realized that the attraction of it all was mainly an emotional voyeurism, as well as the draw of simple gore. A beloved dog stolen, a child murdered, a family terrorized in their own home, a drunk driver killing an innocent pedestrian, a senseless gang slaying, these are the disheartening and discouraging events encountered daily by the "news" watcher. Of course such fare harms our soul, even if we are perversely drawn by the outrage of it all.

One redemptive response is to "pray the news." I found this extremely helpful. If I'm watching the news, and a terrible story comes on, after a moment I will mute the TV and pray for the people victimized by that atrocity. I want to stress, Maria, that this is actually quite an important response. We must not just passively watch human suffering happen; we can call upon the God who cares about people, and ask him to strengthen and encourage those who have been victimized and are suffering. We can ask him to bring justice and healing to their lives, and to help them in this time of great distress. In your prayer, Maria, cite the name of the victim and any other details of specificity. You're not uttering a general prayer into the wind, but a focused intercession on behalf of the person you have just learned about.

Similarly, if a high-speed chase is on, don't just mindlessly watch it, secretly hoping for a wipeout. Pray that no innocent people are harmed, police included, and that the chase would come to a safe and swift end. Of course we may never again hear about the people we've prayed for, but our prayers still matter. God hears them, and it sensitizes us to the suffering of others, and reminds us that we can call upon God to act in our lives and the lives of others. You can pray when you see a police or fire truck speed by with lights and sirens on, and you can pray when you pass the scene of a traffic accident or some other event where people have probably been harmed. God is not indifferent to any human suffering, and we should not be indifferent either. By responding in prayer to stories on the TV or events we see or read about, we remind ourselves that human suffering matters, and we can call upon God's grace anytime, for anyone.

Similarly, music on the radio or a playlist is not meaningless or neutral. Some music is coarse and brutal, some is sweet and inspiring. We know from Scripture that music is very powerful, and central to human experience, and to heaven itself. So we should make it a point to avoid music that coarsens and degrades, rather than ennobles or innocently entertains.

As to podcasts and other media, they can be a chance to "redeem the time," and to learn while doing other tasks like walking or cleaning. We can listen to the Bible read aloud over our cellphone, or we can listen to some other valuable exposition of helpful or important ideas. That's not to say we have to do that every time we use media, but it's wise to think about ways to use media that take advantage of this technology. Contemporary technology enables us to waste more time, or to waste less time, depending on how we employ it.

And of course perhaps the most powerful medium of all, film, is worthy of our reflection. Whether at home or in a theater, to devote about two hours of time to a story replete with powerful images and a soundtrack is to expose ourselves to significant influence. We should think carefully about the movies we watch, and not absentmindedly subject ourselves to them. Human beings are certainly vulnerable to being influenced by what they see and hear.

Behavioral psychology aside, the entire American advertising industry is based on this very premise. I remember lecturing to a group of students in a classroom, and telling them that the gory movie franchise known as *Saw* may not be a good choice for Friday night entertainment. One young man in particular was outraged at this suggestion, and he didn't calm down until I pointed out that television commercials, print ads, and audio ads were all predicated on the knowledge that people's thoughts and actions can be affected by what they see and hear. And all the more so if the images are vivid, shocking, or unusual. He was only mildly deterred from his interest in these sadistic films, but we must be on guard for the desensitizing and brutalizing effect they can have on our psyches.

So, for good or ill, movies can change us. I remember as a teenager being gripped by the Franco Zefferelli TV series *Jesus of Nazareth*. And, like so many others, I recall the power and inspiration of Mel Gibson's film, *The Passion of the Christ*.

So, yes, Maria, you make a very good point when you wonder why we are not more conscious and intentional about what we put before our eyes. If we started each day by resolving to be careful in this regard, or sometimes resolved to go on a "media fast" of a day or so, we would begin to see positive changes in our lives, no doubt. It's amazing to realize that all of the media content we consume and we think we need is in fact something we can do without just fine. After all, for most of human history all the various media we are saturated with today didn't even exist.

SONG TO SAVOR:

"Draw Me Close" by Kelly Carpenter.[2]

PRAYER:

O God, help me to renew my mind and to direct my thoughts in a godly manner. Remind me to be alert to the nature of the images, sounds, and ideas I consume, and lead me to always guard my heart and mind. Empower me to use all kinds of media and information rightly, and may it help me grow and mature.

MEMORIZE:

> I will conduct the affairs of my house with a blameless heart. I will not look with approval on anything that is vile. (Ps 103:2–3)

---

2. Carpenter, "Draw Me Close."

SUGGESTED READING:

Detweiler, Craig. *iGods: How Technology Shapes Our Spiritual and Social Lives.* Grand Rapids: Brazos, 2013.

Muggeridge, Malcolm. *Christ and the Media.* Kent, UK: Hodder & Stoughton, 1977.

Sommerville, C. John. *How the News Makes Us Dumb: The Death of Wisdom in an Information Society.* Downers Grove, IL: InterVarsity, 1999.

Thacker, Jason. *Following Jesus in a Digital Age.* Nashville: B & H, 2022.

Wassom, Brian D. *What Would Jesus Post? Seven Principles Christians Should Follow in Social Media.* Bloomington, IN: Westbow, 2013.

15

Race

"The line separating good and evil passes not through states, nor between classes, nor between political parties either—but right through every human heart."

—Aleksandr Solzhenitsyn

"There are two races of men in this world, but only those two—the 'race' of the decent man and the 'race' of the indecent man. Both are found everywhere; they penetrate into all groups of society. No group consists entirely of decent or indecent people."

—Viktor Frankl

"The United States is the least racist multiracial country in the world. It is probably the best place in the world for a black to live—which is why almost no black Americans have decided to leave America for anywhere, including black Africa."

—Dennis Prager

RACE

From: thebradstetson@gmail.com
To: Ben

Thank you for your passionate note, Ben. Yes, I agree with you: America is racially sick, and Christians are generally not helping our nation recover from its racialist malady. Race obsession is never good, it never leads to socially humane arrangements, and it never leads people to psychological or spiritual health. As I said to you when we spoke briefly after my chapel talk, I'm a "racial individualist," or a racial humanist. Those are just a lot of syllables to reassert Dr. Martin Luther King Jr.'s vision of color blindness, and the primacy of individual character. I oppose collectivist morality and defining oneself by one's racial group. We are each individual human persons, and it is on that basis God understands us.

It is lamentable, to say the least, that socially and culturally we find ourselves in this position. It took our civilization in North America literally centuries to largely surmount bitter, hateful, violent, irrational anti-black racism. And just as so much progress toward color blindness had been made, we've largely reverted to race obsession.

The contours of today's racialism are different than before: we've substantially supplanted the hatred of blacks with a strong cultural contempt, if not outright hatred, of whites; the drive toward "anti-racism" has replaced the goal of color blindness, and racial collectivism is once again the norm over the racial individualism that had been budding since 1968, which I hold was really the victorious end of the Civil Rights Movement. And, Ben, I'm very sorry to say that the Christian churches have done very little to stand against the new racial obsessions, and indeed they even seem to foment them, so often in the name of "racial reconciliation." On the topic of race, so many Christian bodies—left and right—have been totally acculturated, they've become just like the larger culture. They seek to buy a social "innocence," as Shelby Steele puts it, by getting on the cultural bandwagon of racial wokeness and anti-white hostility.[1]

---

1. See Steele, *Content of Our Character*, and also his book *White Guilt*. See also the important book by McWhorter, *Woke Racism*.

Part II: Social and Ethical Topics

I've written before about race, Ben, and even though those books are from a few years ago, I think they still have something valuable to say. Let me summarize them in just a few propositions: The American Left and black grievance groups ridiculously exaggerate about white racism today in order to achieve political and social capital; the greatest enemies to black progress today are inside the black community itself; fatherless-ness is the most significant problem in the black community, and one of the most important social problems in our country writ large; the most underreported story in America today is anti-white racism; Christians have a moral and biblical duty to stand against race consciousness in all its forms.[2]

The literature documenting those first four assertions is voluminous. You might not have heard a lot about it, because you may well get called "racist" for reading those books or talking about them, but they are there, and the case they make is overwhelmingly convincing.[3] So I'd like to comment briefly on the last point above, namely, that Christians have a real, comprehensive obligation to resist race consciousness.

Individualism, Ben, is a deeply biblical idea. Of course we must care profoundly about our community, and serve our community, but God will judge us as individuals, not as members of a group, racial or otherwise. We are fully responsible for our own behavior, not others'. We are called to form our own character in godliness and Christlikeness, encouraged and inspired by the Holy Spirit. Our sanctification is God's work alone, but as I am fond of saying, grace is opposed to earning, not effort. So we can and should do all we can personally to live the gospel, and emulate Jesus in our lives. Individual moral responsibility and a communitarian social concern are not mutually exclusive, and indeed, as believers we are called to both.

---

2. See Conti and Stetson, *Challenging the Civil Rights Establishment*; Faryna et al., *Black and Right*; and Peterson and Stetson, *From Rage to Responsibility*.

3. See also the works of Thomas Sowell, Shelby Steele, and Larry Elder. As well, see the insightful work of Hughes, *End of Race Politics*.

Pastor Vodie Baucham Jr. has written eloquently about race and the dangers of the new anti-racism. His book, *Fault Lines: The Social Justice Movement and Evangelicalism's Looming Catastrophe*, is must-reading. I urge you to read it carefully. Among other points he makes—and he is not the only contemporary writer to make this point—is that the new racialism (which is sometimes called "wokeness," "anti-racism," or "Diversity, Equity, and Inclusion") is essentially religious in character.

Ben, let me quote him at length, as his words of warning are important:

> At the epicenter of the coming evangelical catastrophe is a new religion—or, more specifically, a new cult.... This new cult has created a new lexicon that has served as a scaffolding to support what has become an entire body of divinity. [It comes] with its own cosmology (CT/CRT/I); original sin (racism); law (antiracism); gospel (racial reconciliation); martyrs (Saints Trayvon, Mike, George, Breonna, etc.); priests (oppressed minorities); means of atonement (reparations); new birth (wokeness); liturgy (lament); canon (CSJ social science); theologians (DiAngelo, Kendi, Brown, Krenshaw, etc.); and catechism (say their names).[4]

As Baucham argues throughout his book, this new and growing enthronement of race as god is idolatrous, and personally and socially destructive. It is fully unbiblical. Christians must bear witness to God's love for each individual human being. His love for us does not see skin color or tribal identification, nor is it compromised by the sins of our ancestors. Those are all non-essential traits about us that can get in the way of us loving each other, and of seeing ourselves as first and foremost—and above all—flawed individual persons redeemed by Jesus' suffering, death, and resurrection. Just as God did with young David, he looks upon our hearts, and that is what he values, not our outward appearance (1 Sam 16:7). This isn't a complicated idea, Ben, but

---

4. Baucham Jr., *Fault Lines*, 66–67.

it is countercultural in America today, and so we must vigorously contend for it, even if we are called "racist" for doing so.

You show great courage, Ben, in being willing to talk about this topic. So many people, Christians and otherwise, will just remain quiet, and go along to get along. They are easily bullied into silence. But the poison of race consciousness cannot be tolerated, and people of goodwill today, just as in the past, must stand against it. Obsession with race leads people away from thinking in moral categories, and it foments interpersonal and social hostility. These are destructive forces.

Ben, God will strengthen you and encourage you as you stand for truth and a truly Christian worldview, on all matters, throughout all the seasons of your life. Remember he is always with you and within you.

SONG TO SAVOR:

"All Creatures of Our God and King" by St. Francis of Assisi, adapted by Jonathan Baird and Ryan Baird.[5]

PRAYER:

O God, help me to look on the heart, and not on outward appearance. Teach me to value character over appearance, and to always remember that every individual person is unique and valuable, dignified and bearing your image. Teach me to hate unfairness and injustice, and to stand against it wherever I find it, in whatever form I find it. Amen.

MEMORIZE:

> Then Peter began to speak. "I now realize how true it is that God does not show favoritism, but accepts from every nation the one who fears him and does what is

---

5. Baird and Baird, "All Creatures."

right. You know the message God sent to the people of Israel, announcing the good news of peace through Jesus Christ, who is Lord of all." (Acts 10:34–36)

SUGGESTED READING:

Baucham, Vodie T. Jr. *Fault Lines: The Social Justice Movement and Evangelicalism's Looming Catastrophe.* Washington, DC: Salem, 2022.

Hughes, Coleman. *The End of Race Politics.* New York: Penguin, 2024.

Loury, Glenn C. *Late Admissions: Confessions of a Black Conservative.* New York: Norton, 2024.

Ondaatje, Michael L. *Black Conservative Intellectuals in Modern America.* Philadelphia: University of Pennsylvania Press, 2012.

Steele, Shelby. *A Dream Deferred: The Second Betrayal of Black Freedom in America.* New York: Harper Perennial, 1999.

Appendix A

12 Breath Prayers and Declarations, and a Daily Prayer of Committal

JOHN CALVIN ONCE SAID the Psalms are the anatomy of the soul. These short prayers that can be said in a breath are mostly drawn from the Psalms. As you say these short prayers and declarations throughout the day, and in any circumstance, you will draw strength and encouragement.

1. "Lord Jesus, be my shepherd, and carry me forever." (Based on Ps 28:9.)
2. "May my thoughts and words honor you, O God, today and always." (Based on Ps 19:14.)
3. "God, help me to honor you today, and to trust in you." (Based on Prov 3:5–6.)
4. "Lord, strengthen me and encourage me today." (Based on Ps 46:1.)
5. "God, be my protection, shield, and shelter today." (Based on Ps 119:114.)
6. "For the sake of your name, O Lord, forgive my iniquity though it is great." (Based on Ps 25:11.)

7. "I pray I would decrease, but Christ in me would increase." (Based on John 3:30.)
8. "O Holy Spirit, help me, heal me, teach me, and transform me." (Based on Ps 30:2.)
9. "Protect me, O Lord, from all hurt, harm, or danger today." (Based on Ps 91:7.)
10. "God is God, and I am not." (Based on Isa 45:9.)
11. "Lord Jesus, son of David, have mercy on me, a sinner." (Based on Mark 10:47.)
12. "The Lord is gracious and full of compassion, slow to anger and of great mercy." (Based on Ps 145:8.)

DAILY COMMITTAL PRAYER:

"Lord, I thank you for the life you have given me for this day, and I ask you to help me to use it for your glory. Bring out the best in me today and always, and help me to become all you have intended for me to be. Please forgive me of all my sins and past failures, and help me to look forwards, not backwards, and to honor you in all I do today. Help me to be a good steward of all my talents and resources, and help me to grow in you and towards you each day, and to truly love and forgive all the people you bring into my life. In the name of my Lord and Savior Jesus Christ I pray, amen."

Appendix B

Dietrich Bonhoeffer's Legacy for Americans Today

APRIL 9, 1945, SAW the death by hanging of Dietrich Bonhoeffer, the young German theologian and pastor who led Christian resistance inside Germany against the Nazis. Though only thirty-nine when he was executed on Hitler's direct orders—just three weeks before the dictator's suicide in his Berlin bunker—Bonhoeffer's life and thought are a compelling legacy of moral conscience, reminding us that our faith can demand of us difficult decisions.

In the decades since his murder, Bonhoeffer has regularly—if always implausibly—been drafted by the religious and political left as an exemplar of its latest movement: The romantic and moving story of the young scholar and minister who gave up a life of privilege and safety to "fight the power" of an unjust government has been an attractive banner for those who've flattered themselves into believing they are doing the same. The death of God movement of the 1960s, the liberation theologies of the 1970s, and the thoroughly secularized academic religious studies of the 1980s, nineties, and 2000s each seized on different aspects of Bonhoeffer's thought—his impatience with religiosity, his solidarity with the suffering, his emphasis on human autonomy—in a strained effort to make him their own.

Appendix B

Much more reasonably though, in today's age of deep geopolitical complexity, Americans should see in Bonhoeffer's witness not a call to the barricades, but the simple and sobering personal lesson that amid the apparent (though always divinely superintended) vicissitudes of history, authentic devotion to transcendent truth and opposition to evil may well lead to individual suffering, not succor, and to hardship, not happiness.

In the summer of 1939, with the dark penumbra of Nazi evil quickly growing, Bonhoeffer—at age thirty-three already an accomplished scholar—arrived in the safety of New York City set to teach at the prestigious Union Theological Seminary alongside the renowned Reinhold Niebuhr, who would come to be known as American's theologian of the Cold War. But Bonhoeffer kept the perch less than two months, leaving so abruptly his room was found strewn with his papers and cigarette butts. Bonhoeffer loved Germany and its people, and his conscience had been convinced of the need to come to their aid by actively joining the resistance to Hitler. He later wrote to Niebuhr, explaining his sudden return to Germany, "I made a mistake in coming to America. . . . I shall have no right to take part in the restoration of Christian life in Germany after the war unless I share the trials of this time with my people."[1]

Bonhoeffer's decision was a victory of courage over self-preservation. The Gestapo had already banned the uncooperative pastor from the city of Berlin, and a few months after his return the Gestapo issued an order forbidding Bonhoeffer from speaking in public, and later from printing or publishing. The official German Evangelical Church had become a Nazi organ, and the ominous sounds of *Kristallnacht*—the night of November 10, 1938, when Jewish shops and synagogues across Germany were freely plundered—no doubt rang in his head. It is telling that November 10, 1938, is the only date noted in Bonhoeffer's personal Bible. He knew the murderous myopia gripping German society, and he knew anyone who opposed it might have to pay the ultimate price. Still, he joined the *Abwehr*, the German military intelligence, as a double agent, using the ecumenical contacts he had developed

---

1. Young III, *No Difference in the Fare*, 39.

across Europe to publicize the resistance movement, gain foreign support for it, and ultimately conduct "Operation 7," an attempt to spirit Jews into Switzerland. It was this latter activity, along with the later Nazi realization that Bonhoeffer had been a knowing participant in the planning of a 1944 assassination attempt against Hitler, that sealed his fate.

After his arrest in April of 1943, Bonhoeffer studied, prayed, wrote, and ministered to other prisoners incarcerated with him at the Flossenburg Concentration Camp in Bavaria. His posthumously published *Letters and Papers from Prison* show an active mind and a pastoral heart. And yet, although he was spiritually and intellectually immensely productive in those final two years— he wrote to his parents that in prison he was learning to practice himself what he had said to other people in sermons and books— he was at times restless and fearful.[2]

Yet he never regretted his work against the Nazi machine. Bonhoeffer had long been a pacifist, but beholding the nature and scope of Nazism led him to abandon his idealistic stance. When a fellow prisoner once asked him how he could have been a part of a plan to murder someone, Bonhoeffer explained that if he, as a Christian pastor, saw a drunken driver speeding through a street full of people, his primary duty was not to bury the victims and comfort the bereaved, but to do whatever he could to wrench the wheel away from the drunken madman.

In prison Bonhoeffer struggled with depression and self-doubt, though he knew that the other prisoners and even the guards were impressed with him. They had told him he stepped from his cell like a squire from his country house, like someone who was accustomed to always winning. But compliments to vanity were no comfort to a serious man increasingly sensing his grim fate, confined in his own gray Gethsemane. Bonhoeffer felt frustrated by his situation, embarrassed by the gap between how brave he seemed outwardly and how weak he felt inwardly, and he was pained by the paradox of his precocious, promising life coming to a seemingly anonymous, unfulfilling ending.

2. Bethge, *Dietrich Bonhoeffer*, 119–21.

Appendix B

    Remembering Pastor Bonhoeffer's martyrdom for God and good, Christians in America today and all people of goodwill can claim him as their own as well, and find in his unyielding devotion to truth over tyranny and freedom over fascism the strength of character to personally and conscientiously confront the evils of their own life and time, whatever they may be, no matter the cost.

Bibliography

Anderson, Neil T., et al. *Freedom From Addiction.* Ventura, CA: Regal, 1996.
Anderson, Neil T. *Winning the Battle Within: Realistic Steps to Overcoming Sexual Strongholds.* Eugene, OR: Harvest House, 2008.
Aniol, Scott. *Worship in Song: A Biblical Philosophy of Music and Worship.* Winona Lake, IN: BMH, 2009.
Arnold, Clinton. *Powers of Darkness: Principalities and Powers in Paul's Letters.* Downers Grove, IL: InterVarsity, 1992.
Arterburn, Stephen, and Fred Stoeker. *Every Young Man's Battle: Strategies for Victory in the Real World of Sexual Temptation.* Colorado Springs, CO: Waterbrook, 2002.
Arterburn, Stephen, and David Stoop. *Understanding and Loving a Person with Alcohol and Drug Addiction.* Colorado Springs, CO: David C. Cook, 2018.
Baird, Jonathan, and Ryan Baird. "All Creatures of Our God and King." Originally written by Francis of Assisi. On *Prayers of the Saints.* Integrity Music and Sovereign Grace Music, 2017. Uploaded to YouTube, January 4, 2018. https://www.youtube.com/watch?v=MUZDohgtSgE&list=RDMUZDohgtSgE&start_radio=1.
Baucham, Vodie T. Jr. *Fault Lines: The Social Justice Movement and Evangelicalism's Looming Catastrophe.* Washington, DC: Salem, 2022.
Beckwith, Francis. *Abortion and the Sanctity of Human Life.* Joplin, MO: College Press, 2000.
———. *Defending Life: A Moral and Legal Case Against Abortion.* Cambridge: Cambridge University Press, 2007.
———. *Politically Correct Death.* Grand Rapids: Baker, 1993.
Berger, Peter. *A Rumor of Angels.* New York: Doubleday, 1969.
Bethge, Eberhard, ed. *Dietrich Bonhoeffer: Letters and Papers From Prison.* New York: Macmillan, 1971.
Boa, Andrew A. *Redeemed Sexuality: Healing and Transformation in Community.* Downers Grove, IL: InterVarsity, 2017.
Branch, Taylor. *Parting the Waters.* New York: Simon & Schuster, 1989.

Bibliography

Brown, Michael L. *The Power of Music: God's Call to Change the World One Song at a Time*. Lake Mary, FL: Charisma, 2019.

Bultmann, Rudolf. *New Testament and Mythology and Other Basic Writings*. Minneapolis: Fortress, 1984.

Carpenter, Kelly. "Draw Me Close." On *Draw Me Close*. Released 2001. Uploaded to YouTube by McDoju, October 22, 2011. https://www.youtube.com/watch?v=L9h7fuL18vI&list=RDL9h7fuL18vI&start_radio=1.

Casting Crowns. "Scars in Heaven." Written by Mark Hall and Matthew West. On *Healer*. Provident Music Group, 2021. Official music video uploaded to YouTube, June 4, 2021. https://www.youtube.com/watch?v=qCdevloDE6E.

Chan, Sam. *Evangelism in a Skeptical World: How to Make the Unbelievable News About Jesus More Believable*. Grand Rapids: Zondervan, 2018.

Cloud, Henry, and John Townsend. *Boundaries in Dating: How Healthy Choices Grow Healthy Relationships*. Grand Rapids: Zondervan, 2000.

Conti, Joseph G., and Brad Stetson. *Challenging the Civil Rights Establishment: Profiles of a New Black Vanguard*. Westport, CT: Praeger, 1993.

Dallas Willard Ministries. "Apologetics in Action." https://dwillard.org/resources/articles/apologetics-in-action.

Demarest, Bruce A. *The Cross and Salvation: The Doctrine of Salvation*. Wheaton, IL: Crossway, 2006.

Detweiler, Craig. *iGods: How Technology Shapes Our Spiritual and Social Lives*. Grand Rapids: Brazos, 2013.

Doerksen, Brian. "At the Cross." On *Resurrection Celebration*. Vineyard Music, 1994. Uploaded to YouTube by AsTheDeer, Dec. 7, 2009. https://www.youtube.com/watch?v=m5rmIckeEgQ.

Douthat, Ross. *Believe*. Grand Rapids: Zondervan, 2025.

Dreher, Rod. *Live Not by Lies: A Manual for Christian Dissidents*. New York: Sentinel, 2022.

———. *Living in Wonder: Finding Mystery and Meaning in a Secular Age*. Grand Rapids: Zondervan, 2024.

Duke Health. "Study Shows Impact of Paternal Marijuana Exposure on the Brains of Offspring." February 24, 2020. https://corporate.dukehealth.org/news/study-shows-impact-paternal-marijuana-exposure-brains-offspring.

Elliot, Elisabeth. *Suffering Is Never for Nothing*. Nashville: B&H, 2019.

Ellwood, Robert S. *Introducing Religion from the Inside and Outside*. Upper Saddle River, NJ: Prentice-Hall, 1978.

Elmore, Robert. "The Place of Music in Christian Life." *Christianity Today*, January 31, 1964. https://www.christianitytoday.com/1964/01/place-of-music-in-christian-life/.

Faryna, Stan, et al., eds. *Black and Right: The Bold New Voice of Black Conservatives in America*. Westport, CT: Praeger, 1997.

Fields, Leslie Leyland, and Jill Hubbard. *Forgiving Our Fathers and Mothers: Finding Freedom From Hurt and Hate*. Nashville: Thomas Nelson, 2014.

Bibliography

Francis, James Allen. *The Real Jesus, and Other Sermons*. Philadelphia: Judson, 1926.

Getty, Keith, and Kristyn Getty. "I Am Not My Own." Written by Skye Peterson et al. On *Christ Our Hope in Life and Death*. Getty Music, 2023. Lyric video uploaded to YouTube, Febuary 23, 2023. https://www.youtube.com/watch?v=yxCb6l3jkis.

———. "In Christ Alone." Written by Stuart Townsend and Keith Getty. Released 2001. Lyric video uploaded to YouTube, January 11, 2024. https://www.youtube.com/watch?v=m_063OI38RQ.

Got Questions. "Does the Bible Support the Pre-Existence of Jesus?" https://www.gotquestions.org/pre-existence-Jesus.html.

Green, Keith. "Create in Me a Clean Heart." On *Keith Green Easter Collection*. Produced by Last Days Ministries. Sparrow Records, 1990. Uploaded to YouTube, March 28, 2024. https://www.youtube.com/watch?v=-CLbw5jdKoo.

Greig, Pete. *How to Pray: A Simple Guide for Normal People*. Colorado Springs, CO: NavPress, 2019.

Grimstead, Gregory B. *The Hidden Promise, Honoring Your Parents: A Christian Perspective on How, Why and When to Honor Your Parents*. Scotts Valley, CA: CreateSpace, 2014.

Grudem, Wayne. *Systematic Theology*. 2nd ed. Grand Rapids: Zondervan, 2020.

Guthrie, Nancy. *Holding On to Hope: A Pathway Through Suffering to the Heart of God*. Carol Stream, IL: Tyndale, 2002.

Hansen, Collin. "Ravi Zacharias and the Judgment of God." The Gospel Coalition, February 12, 2021. https://www.thegospelcoalition.org/article/ravi-zacharias-judgment-god/?queryID=dd3a04cde13880dbe848a8adf4cbf506.

Heiser, Michael S. *Demons: What the Bible Really Says About the Powers of Darkness*. Bellingham, WA: Lexham, 2020.

———. *Supernatural: What the Bible Teaches About the Unseen World—and Why It Matters*. Bellingham, WA: Lexham, 2015.

Hughes, Coleman. *The End of Race Politics*. New York: Penguin, 2024.

Jones, E. Michael. *Degenerate Moderns: Modernity as Rationalized Sexual Misbehavior*. San Francisco: Ignatius, 1993.

Jones, Rachel K., and Amy Friedrich-Karnik. "Medication Abortion Accounted for 63% of All US Abortions in 2023—An Increase from 53% in 2020." Guttmacher, March 19, 2024. https://www.guttmacher.org/2024/03/medication-abortion-accounted-63-all-us-abortions-2023-increase-53-2020.

Keller, Timothy. *Prayer: Experiencing Awe and Intimacy with God*. New York: Penguin, 2016.

———. *Walking with God Through Pain and Suffering*. New York: Penguin, 2015.

Bibliography

Keller, Timothy, and Kathy Keller. *The Meaning of Marriage: Facing the Complexities of Commitment with the Wisdom of God.* New York: Penguin, 2013.

Kendrick, Graham, and Robin Mark. "All I Once Held Dear (Knowing You)." On *The Mandate—Experiencing God.* Integrity Music, 2003. Uploaded to YouTube by boaztsai, August 26, 2010. https://www.youtube.com/watch?v=oxpPIa-BskY.

Klusendorf, Scott. *The Case for Life: Equipping Christians to Engage the Culture.* Wheaton, IL: Crossway, 2009.

Lague, Ian, ed. "Abortion in the United States." Guttmacher, April 2025. Updated by Isaac Maddow-Zimet and Emma Stoskopf-Ehrlich. https://www.guttmacher.org/fact-sheet/induced-abortion-united-states.

Latorre, Chelsea. "How Music Affects Your Mood." West Virginia University Carruth Center, March 5, 2019. https://carruth.wvu.edu/carruth-blog/2019/03/05/how-music-affects-your-mood.

Lefebvre, Michael. *Singing the Songs of Jesus: Revisiting the Psalms.* Fearn: Christian Focus, 2011.

Levitin, Daniel. *I Heard There Was a Secret Chord: Music as Medicine.* New York: Norton, 2024.

Lewis, C. S. *How to Pray.* San Francisco: HarperOne, 2018.

———. *Mere Christianity.* Deluxe ed. New York: HarperOne, 2025.

———. *The Screwtape Letters.* New York: Macmillan, 1961.

Loury, Glenn C. *Late Admissions: Confessions of a Black Conservative.* New York: Norton, 2024.

Lowery, David. *Following Jesus in an Age of Hypocrisy.* Eugene, OR: Wipf & Stock, 2020.

Luther, Martin. "A Mighty Fortress Is Our God." 1529. Translated by Frederic Henry Hedge, 1852. Hymnary.org. https://hymnary.org/text/a_mighty_fortress_is_our_god_a_bulwark.

Lutzer, Erwin. *The Power of a Clear Conscience: Let God Free You from Your Past.* Eugene, OR: Harvest House, 2016.

———. *We Will Not Be Silenced: Responding Courageously to Our Culture's Assault on Christianity.* Eugene, OR: Harvest House, 2020.

Lynch, Danielle Anne. *God in Sound and Silence: Music as Theology.* Eugene, OR: Pickwick, 2018.

MacArthur, John. *Alone With God: Rediscovering the Power and Passion of Prayer.* Colorado Springs, CO: David C. Cook, 2011.

March of Dimes. "Stillbirth." https://www.marchofdimes.org/find-support/topics/miscarriage-loss-grief/stillbirth.

Markos, Louis. *Apologetics for the Twenty-First Century.* Wheaton, IL: Crossway, 2010.

Martins, Carlos. *The Exorcist Files.* Brentwood, TN: Faithwords, 2024.

Matthews, Dale A., and Connie Clark. *The Faith Factor: Proof of the Healing Power of Prayer.* New York: Penguin, 1999.

McDowell, Josh. *The New Evidence That Demands a Verdict.* Nashville: Thomas Nelson, 1999.

Bibliography

McWhorter, John. *Woke Racism: How a New Religion Has Betrayed Black America*. New York: Portfolio, 2021.

Midori, Natashia. "Still." Written by Reuben Morgan. On *Thank You Jesus, Pt. 1*, released 2016. Lyric video uploaded to YouTube, January 29, 2019. https://www.youtube.com/watch?v=SXG-ENFAvl8.

Montgomery, John Warwick. *Faith Founded on Fact*. Nashville: Thomas Nelson, 1978.

———. *History and Christianity*. Minneapolis: Bethany House, 1986.

Moon, Jay W., and W. Bud Simon. *Effective Intercultural Evangelism: Good News in a Diverse World*. Downers Grove, IL: InterVarsity, 2021.

Moreland, J. P. *Scaling the Secular City*. Grand Rapids: Zondervan, 1987.

Moreland, J. P., and Norman Geisler. *The Life and Death Debate: Moral Issues of Our Time*. Westport, CT: Greenwood, 1990.

Muggeridge, Malcolm. *Christ and the Media*. Kent, UK: Hodder & Stoughton, 1977.

Murray, Andrew. *With Christ in the School of Prayer*. New York: Fleming Revell, 1895.

Neuhaus, Richard John. *The Naked Public Square: Religion and Democracy in America*. Grand Rapids: Eerdmans, 1988.

Newbigin, Leslie. *The Gospel in a Pluralist Society*. Grand Rapids: Eerdmans, 1989.

Northrup, Lanier T. *When God Calls You to Recovery: Using the Lord's Strength to Break and Destroy Addiction*. Tulsa, OK: Trilogy Christian, 2020.

O'Malley, Patrick, and Tim Madigan. *Getting Grief Right: Finding Your Story of Love in the Sorrow of Loss*. Louisville, CO: Sounds True, 2017.

Ondaatje, Michael L. *Black Conservative Intellectuals in Modern America*. Philadelphia: University of Pennsylvania Press, 2012.

Packer, J. I. *Evangelism and the Sovereignty of God*. Downers Grove, IL: InterVarsity, 2012.

Packer J. I., and Carolyn Nystrom. *Prayer: Finding Our Way Through Duty to Delight*. Downers Grove, IL: InterVarsity, 2009.

Pasulka, Diana. *American Cosmic: UFOs, Religion, Technology*. New York: Oxford University Press, 2019.

———. *Encounters: Experiences with Nonhuman Intelligences*. New York: St. Martin's, 2023.

Pearcey, Nancy R. *Love Thy Body: Answering Hard Questions About Life and Sexuality*. Grand Rapids: Baker, 2018.

Peterson, Eugene H. *A Long Obedience in the Same Direction: Discipleship in an Instant Society*. Commemorative ed. Downers Grove, IL: InterVarsity, 2024.

Peterson, Jesse Lee, and Brad Stetson. *From Rage to Responsibility: Black Conservative Jesse Lee Peterson and America Today*. St. Paul: Paragon House, 2000.

The Porter's Gate. "Christ Is Lower Still." Performed by The Porter's Gate, Matt Maher, and DOE. On *Sanctuary Songs*. The Porter's Gate, 2023. Uploaded to YouTube, September 7, 2023. https://www.youtube.com/watch?v=_G5UoNDxdxU.

Bibliography

Prager, Dennis. "What's Causing Pandemic of Adult Children Who Won't Ever Again Speak to Their Parents?" The Daily Signal, July 14, 2023. https://www.dailysignal.com/2023/07/14/postmodern-pandemic-cruelty/.

Redman, Matt. "Heart of Worship." On *The Heart of Worship*. WorshipTogether, 1999. Lyric video uploaded to YouTube, May 19, 2023. https://www.youtube.com/watch?v=gljs4N7ZoD4.

Reeves, Michael. *Evangelical Pharisees: The Gospel as Cure for the Church's Hypocrisy*. Wheaton, IL: Crossway, 2023.

Renn, Aaron M. *Life in the Negative World*. Grand Rapids: Zondervan, 2024.

Reno, R. R. *Resurrecting the Idea of a Christian Society*. Nashville: Salem, 2016.

Scroggins, Jimmy, et al. *Turning Everyday Conversations into Gospel Conversations*. Nashville: B & H, 2016.

Shaw, Mark E. *The Heart of Addiction*. Bemidji, MN: Focus, 2008.

Shroff, Lila. "ChatGPT Gave Instructions for Murder, Self-Mutilation, and Devil Worship." The Atlantic, July 24, 2025. https://www.theatlantic.com/technology/archive/2025/07/chatgpt-ai-self-mutilation-satanism/683649/.

Simonds, Wendy. *Abortion at Work: Ideology and Practice in a Feminist Clinic*. New Brunswick, NJ: Rutgers University Press, 1996.

Sittser, Gerald. *A Grace Disguised: How the Soul Grows Through Loss*. Grand Rapids: Zondervan, 1996.

Slattery, Juli. *Rethinking Sexuality: God's Design and Why It Matters*. Colorado Springs, CO: Multnomah, 2018.

Smith, Michael, arr. "A Mighty Fortress Is Our God." Originally written by Martin Luther. On *The Hymns*. Rocketown Records, 2019. Uploaded to YouTube by Michael W. Smith, October 9, 2019. https://www.youtube.com/watch?v=-ZwFSBxyL5c.

Sommerville, C. John. *How the News Makes Us Dumb: The Death of Wisdom in an Information Society*. Downers Grove, IL: InterVarsity, 1999.

Stanley, Charles. *5 Things to Pray for Your Parents: Prayers That Change Things for an Older Generation*. Charlotte, NC: Good Book, 2012.

Stanton, Glenn T. "Ten Things Everyone Should Know About a Christian Sexual Ethic." Focus on the Family Canada, December 17, 2014. https://www.focusonthefamily.ca/content/ten-things-everyone-should-know-about-a-christian-sexual-ethic.

Steele, Shelby. *The Content of Our Character: A New Vision of Race in America*. New York: Harper Perennial, 1998.

———. *A Dream Deferred: The Second Betrayal of Black Freedom in America*. New York: Harper Perennial, 1999.

———. *White Guilt: How Blacks and Whites Together Destroyed the Promise of the Civil Rights Era*. New York: Harper Perennial, 2007.

Stetson, Brad. *Living Victims, Stolen Lives: Parents of Murdered Children Speak to America*. New York: Routledge, 2003.

———. *Pluralism and Particularity in Religious Belief*. Westport, CT: Praeger, 1996.

———. *Tender Fingerprints: A True Story of Loss and Resolution.* Grand Rapids: Zondervan, 1999.

Stetson, Brad, ed. *Choosing to Survive: Loved Ones of Murder Victims Tell Their Stories.* Omaha, NE: Centering, 2017.

———. *The Silent Subject: Reflections on the Unborn in American Culture.* Westport, CT: Praeger, 1996.

Stetson, Brad, and Joseph G. Conti. *The Truth About Tolerance: Pluralism, Diversity and the Culture Wars.* Downers Grove, IL: InterVarsity, 2005.

Stoop, David. *Forgiving Our Parents, Forgiving Ourselves: The Definitive Guide.* Grand Rapids: Fleming Revell, 2011.

Strobel, Lee. *The Case for Christ.* Grand Rapids: Zondervan, 1998.

———. *The Case for Faith.* Grand Rapids: Zondervan, 2006.

Sullivan, Randall. *The Devil's Best Trick: How the Face of Evil Disappeared.* New York: Atlantic Monthly, 2024.

Ten Elshof, Gregg. *I Told Me So: Self-Deception and the Christian Life.* Grand Rapids: Eerdmans, 2009.

Thacker, Jason. *Following Jesus in a Digital Age.* Nashville: B & H, 2022.

Thomas, Gary L. *Sacred Marriage: What If God Designed Marriage to Make Us Holy More Than to Make Us Happy?* Grand Rapids: Zondervan, 2015.

———. *The Sacred Search: What If It's Not About Who You Marry, But Why?* Colorado Springs, CO: David C. Cook, 2013.

Tolson, Chester L., and Harold G. Koenig. *The Healing Power of Prayer: The Surprising Connection Between Prayer and Your Health.* Grand Rapids: Baker, 2004.

Tomlin, Chris. "Good Good Father." Written by Tony Brown and Pat Barrett. On *Never Lose Sight.* Sixsteprecords, 2016. Uploaded to YouTube by christomlinmusic, October 2, 2016. https://www.youtube.com/watch?v=CqybaIesbuA&list=RDCqybaIesbuA&start_radio=1.

Trobisch, Walter. *I Married You.* North Collins, NY: Quiet Waters, 1971.

Trueman, Carl R. *Grace Alone—Salvation as a Gift of God.* Grand Rapids: Zondervan, 2017.

———. *The Rise and Triumph of the Modern Self.* Wheaton, IL: Crossway, 2020.

Volkow, Nora D., et al. "Adverse Health Effects of Marijuana Use." *New England Journal of Medicine* 370 (2014) 2219–27. https://www.nejm.org/doi/10.1056/NEJMra1402309.

Vroegop, Mark. *Dark Clouds, Deep Mercy: Discovering the Grace of Lament.* Wheaton, IL: Crossway, 2019.

Walls, Jerry. *Hell: The Logic of Damnation.* South Bend, IN: University of Notre Dame Press, 1992.

Walsh, Matt. *Church of Cowards: A Wake-Up Call to Complacent Christians.* Washington DC: Regnery, 2022.

Wassom, Brian D. *What Would Jesus Post? Seven Principles Christians Should Follow in Social Media.* Bloomington, IN: Westbow, 2013.

Bibliography

Watts, Isaac. "When I Survey the Wondrous Cross." 1707. Arranged and recorded by Nathan Drake. On *Hymns of the Son*. Reawaken Hymns. Lyric video uploaded to YouTube by Reawaken Hymns, May 10, 2022. https://www.youtube.com/watch?v=7rEpweSCR0Y.

Welch, Edward T. *Addictions: A Banquet in the Grave*. Phillipsburg, NJ: P & R, 2001.

Wellum, Stephen J. *God the Son Incarnate*. Wheaton, IL: Crossway, 2016.

Wickham, Phil. "It's Always Been You." On *Hymn of Heaven*. Fair Trade Services and Columbia Records, 2021. Uploaded to YouTube by Phil Wickham, May 13, 2021. https://www.youtube.com/watch?v=58pBvQaoXSM&list=RD58pBvQaoXSM&start_radio=1.

Willard, Dallas. "Apologetics in Action." Interview with *Cutting Edge Magazine*. Dallas Willard Ministries, 2001. https://dwillard.org/resources/articles/apologetics-in-action.

———. *The Divine Conspiracy: Rediscovering Our Hidden Life in God*. San Francisco: HarperOne, 1998.

———. *Hearing God: Developing a Conversational Relationship with God*. Downers Grove, IL: InterVarsity, 2012.

———. *Renovation of the Heart*. Colorado Springs, CO: NavPress, 2002.

———. *The Spirit of the Disciplines: Understanding How God Changes Lives*. San Francisco: HarperOne, 1999.

Wright, N. T., and Michael F. Bird. *Jesus and the Powers: Christian Political Witness in an Age of Totalitarian Terror and Dysfunctional Democracies*. Grand Rapids: Zondervan, 2024.

Yep, Jeanette, et al., eds. *Following Jesus Without Dishonoring Your Parents*. Downers Grove, IL: InterVarsity, 1998.

Young, Josiah Ulysses III. *No Difference in the Fare: Dietrich Bonhoeffer and the Problem of Racism*. Grand Rapids: Eerdmans, 1998.

Zaatar, Muriel T., et al. "The Transformative Power of Music: Insights into Neuroplasticity, Health, and Disease." *Brain, Behavior, and Immunity* 35 (2024). https://doi.org/10.1016/j.bbih.2023.100716.

ZA Blog. "The Nicene Creed: Where It Came from and Why It Still Matters." Zondervan Academic, March 9, 2018. https://zondervanacademic.com/blog/the-nicene-creed-where-it-came-from-and-why-it-still-matters.

www.ingramcontent.com/pod-product-compliance
Lightning Source LLC
Chambersburg PA
CBHW071330190426
43193CB00041B/1380